FRESH CHINESE

WYNNIE CHAN

METRO BOOKS
NEW YORK

To Li Li and Timmy, for their enthusiasm about new foods.

Note

The Food and Drug Administration advises that eggs should not be consumed raw. This book contains dishes made with raw or lightly cooked eggs. It is prudent for vulnerable people such as pregnant and nursing mothers, invalids, the elderly, babies, and young children to avoid uncooked or lightly cooked dishes made with eggs. Once prepared, these dishes should be kept refrigerated and used promptly.

This book includes dishes made with nuts and nut derivatives. It is advisable for customers with known allergic reactions to nuts and nut derivatives and those who may be potentially vulnerable to these allergies, such as pregnant and nursing mothers, invalids, the elderly, babies, and children to avoid dishes made with nuts and nut oils. It is also prudent to check the labels of pre-prepared ingredients for the possible inclusion of nut derivatives.

Ovens should be preheated to the specified temperature—if using a fan-assisted oven, follow the manufacturer's directions for adjusting the time and the temperature.

Metro Books
122 Fifth Avenue
New York, NY 10011

ISBN-13: 978-1-4351-0067-1
ISBN-10: 1-4531-0067-0

Printed and bound in China

10 9 8 7 6 5 4 3 2 1

Contents

Foreword by Ken Hom

Cardiovascular ailments such as heart disease and strokes are the main cause of death in the UK, and according to figures from the British Heart Foundation they account for more than 235,000 victims every year. One reason for such a high rate is that our diets are high in saturated fat but low in fruit and vegetables.

Traditionally, the Chinese diet is low in fat and high in fruit and vegetables, so the fact that its popularity among the UK population has grown enormously over the past 50 years should be beneficial. According to a study published by the Institute of Grocery Distribution in 2002, Chinese food (including takeouts, ready meals, and restaurant meals) is the most popular ethnic cuisine in the UK and is preferred by 58 percent of consumers. However, bad Chinese takeout food is greasy and unhealthy and is also high in salt and monosodium glutamate (MSG), factors that may increase our risk of cardiovascular problems.

Recognizing the need to encourage the adoption of a healthier diet, the British Heart Foundation in collaboration with the Chinese National Healthy Living Centre in London set up the Chinese Takeaway Project. The aim of the project was to improve the nutritional knowledge of takeout cooks while reinforcing the values of traditional healthy Chinese practices through free training sessions across the country. Training was conducted by Wynnie Chan, a Cantonese-speaking nutritionist, who emphasized the importance of better cooking methods, such as limiting the use of fat and salt, eliminating MSG and food colorings, and encouraging the use of more fruit and vegetables and leaner cuts of meat. The development of healthier versions of popular Chinese takeout dishes, such as sweet and sour pork, chicken chow mein, aromatic crispy duck, and beef in black bean sauce, meant that these and other healthier options became available in many takeout shops. In addition, by using better cooking practices and healthier ingredients takeout food was brought closer to its true source.

Here is a book that contains simple-to-follow recipes with details of the nutritional content of each recipe, such as the amount of fat, calories, and sodium. This means that you can plan and choose dishes that fit in with your lifestyle, whether you are someone who wants to lose weight, a busy mother who needs to feed her family quick, healthy meals, or someone who just loves eating Chinese food. What could be better?

Introduction

The press portrays two very different views of Chinese food—some claim that it is unhealthy because it is full of fat, salt, and MSG, while others believe that the Chinese diet is healthy and nutritious because it uses lots of vegetables and a minimum of oil. Whichever school of belief you support, the aim of this book is to show you that Chinese food, if cooked properly, can be healthy and delicious. Food should be enjoyed, and eating a balanced diet is important for preventing disease and maintaining health.

Traditionally, the Chinese diet was based around vegetables and grain foods, such as rice and noodles, with meats and high-fat foods used as garnishes and flavorings rather than as the main ingredients. There is increasing scientific evidence to show that this type of low-fat, high-fiber diet is very beneficial as it is linked to a lower risk of obesity, heart disease, diabetes, and some cancers.

As countries have become more industrialized and Westernized, the proportions of foods that we eat have changed so that we now have an overemphasis on foods that are high in fat, salt, and protein. The recipes in *Fresh Chinese* aim to redress some of the imbalance by bringing things back to basics, reducing the amount of salt, fat, and sugar while increasing the amount of fruit and vegetables in most dishes—and all without compromising on taste.

WYNNIE CHAN

The Chinese National Healthy Living Centre in London has been active in promoting the health of both the Chinese and British population in the UK through a range of initiatives. The Chinese Healthy Takeaway Project is one such initiative, co-funded by the British Heart Foundation, the New Opportunities Fund, and the Chinese Takeaway Association. This project aims to teach chefs across the UK the principles of healthy cooking, to reinforce traditional good cooking practices, and to encourage healthier alternatives to standard items on their menus.

The inspiration for this book arose as a direct result of this project. The Chinese National Healthy Living Centre is pleased to have been able to support the development of the recipes in this book.

EDDIE CHAN, DIRECTOR, CHINESE NATIONAL HEALTHY LIVING CENTRE, UK

Eating for good health

Following a healthy and balanced diet is enjoyable and easy to achieve. You only really need to know that foods are divided into five main groups, and that a balanced diet is based on eating foods from each group in the right proportions.

The five food groups

These are breads, cereals, and potatoes; fruit and vegetables; milk and dairy foods; meat, fish, and other sources of protein; and sources of sugar and fat.

BREAD, CEREALS, AND POTATOES This group is rich in starchy carbohydrates and includes breakfast cereals, rice, pasta, noodles, yams and oats. It should form the basis of most of your meals. Foods in this group are rich sources of insoluble fiber, calcium, iron, and B vitamins, which are needed to keep your gut, bones, and blood healthy. Try to eat wholegrain, wholemeal, or high-fiber versions whenever you can.

FRUIT AND VEGETABLES This group is an important source of antioxidants, such as vitamin C and beta-carotene (the vegetable equivalent of vitamin A), which help protect us from life-threatening diseases such as cancers and heart disease. Fruits and vegetables are also rich in soluble fiber, which can help to reduce blood cholesterol. Try to include five portions of fruit and vegetables each day—they do not all have to be fresh or organic, although that is ideal, and can include frozen, canned, and dried versions, as well as juices.

A portion of fruit is equivalent to: 1 slice of a very large fruit, e.g., melon, mango, or pineapple ‖ 1 avocado or grapefruit ‖ 1 medium fruit, e.g., banana, pear, apple, or orange ‖ 2 small fruits, e.g., clementines, apricots, kiwi fruit, or plums ‖ 1 cup of very small fruit, e.g., grapes or strawberries ‖ 2–3 tablespoons of canned fruit in natural unsweetened juice, e.g., lychees or peaches ‖ 1 tablespoon of dried fruit, e.g., raisins or dates ‖ ⅔ cup of fresh fruit juice

A portion of vegetables is equivalent to: 2 tablespoons of broccoli, Chinese leaves, zucchini, spinach, cabbage, carrots, corn, shiitake mushrooms, or bok choy ‖ 1 dessert bowlful of salad ‖ 1 cup of sprouted beans ‖ ⅔ cup of fresh vegetable juice

MILK AND DAIRY FOODS This group provides essential nutrients, such as calcium and protein, as well as vitamins A, D, and B12, which are important for maintaining the health of your bones, skin, and blood. Try to include a couple of servings from this group every day and choose low-fat options if possible. Chinese people (except those in northern regions of China) do not generally include dairy foods in their everyday diet. Their main sources of calcium are tofu, bony fish, green leafy vegetables, and calcium-fortified soy milk.

MEAT, FISH, AND PROTEIN ALTERNATIVES The nutrients supplied by this food group include iron, protein, B vitamins, and magnesium, which are needed to maintain healthy blood and efficient functioning of the immune system. Choose a maximum of two servings each day from: lean red meat, fish, chicken, turkey, eggs, nuts, beans, and pulses. Beans and pulses, such as black-eyed beans, mung beans, fava beans, and lentils, make great protein alternatives, as do tofu and bean curd.

FOODS CONTAINING SUGAR AND FOODS CONTAINING FAT Try to keep foods such as savory snacks, cookies, cakes, chips, pastries, candies, chocolate, pies, butter, and carbonated drinks to a minimum, as these contain high levels of fat and/or refined sugar. They are therefore high in calories and can hinder your efforts to lose weight. They also often contain additives such as artificial flavoring, coloring, and preservatives, which are harmful and upset the body's natural balance.

Tips to reduce the amount of fat in your diet **ONE** Choose leaner cuts of meat whenever you can—for example, buy pork loin instead of spareribs. **TWO** Trim any visible fat from meat and poultry either before or after cooking—for example, remove the skin from chicken and duck. **THREE** Steam foods instead of frying or deep-frying them. **FOUR** Skim the fat from the surface of stocks and sauces made from meat or poultry. **FIVE** Cut down on the amount of oil you use for stir-frying. One tablespoon of oil is more than enough when stir-frying a meal for four. **SIX** Always use a spoon to measure oil rather than pouring it directly from a bottle. This way you will know exactly how much you are using. **SEVEN** Use a nonstick sauté or griddle pan so you can cut down on the amount of oil you use. **EIGHT** Choose low-fat versions of products when available—for example, reduced-fat coconut milk, peanut butter, or soy milk.

What about sugar?

Although all fruit and vegetables contain natural sugars, it is the refined sugars that are hidden in many foods, from ades to ready-made meals, which can cause particular problems. Often we do not realize how much sugar we are consuming, so be aware of how much sugar bought food products may contain by checking the list of ingredients on the package. Ideally, cook your own meals using natural ingredients.

Tips to reduce the amount of sugar in your diet **ONE** Choose sugar-free or low-calorie fruit drinks. **TWO** Experiment by cutting down on the amount of sugar you add to your marinades or in cooking. **THREE** Reduced-sugar and low-sugar foods can be helpful aids in the kitchen—for example, choose fruit that has been canned in its natural juice rather than in syrup. **FOUR** Choose fresh fruit for dessert rather than a sticky, sweet pie.

What about salt?

While we all need a small amount of salt (sodium chloride) for our body to function efficiently, we are eating far too much. Scientific studies among the adult population have shown that a high level of salt is associated with high blood pressure or hypertension, and that people with high blood pressure are three times more likely to develop heart disease and strokes.

Tips to reduce the amount of salt in your diet **ONE** Flavor foods with herbs and spices, such as ginger, garlic, cilantro, Szechwan peppercorns, star anise, scallions, chili, and lemon grass, instead of salt. **TWO** Limit the amount of bottled sauces you use—for example, soy sauce, yellow bean sauce, or hoisin sauce. If you're used to dolloping a heaped tablespoon of oyster sauce on your vegetables, you can easily reduce the amount simply by leveling off the tablespoon, and you probably won't even notice the difference. **THREE** Bouillon cubes contain salt and some also contain monosodium glutamate as a flavor enhancer. Whenever possible make your own stocks and use these to enhance and enrich the taste of foods. This will also help you to reduce the amount of salt and bottled sauces you use in your cooking. Freezing small quantities of homemade stock in freezer bags ensures that you will always have an emergency supply without having to resort to a package. **FOUR** Don't add salt to the cooking water for vegetables or rice—you don't need it. If you want to, you can use stock instead. **FIVE** Japanese tamari sauce is much more concentrated than Chinese soy sauce, which means that you need to use only a small amount. Low-sodium alternatives, such as shoyu sauce or low-sodium salt, can be helpful but should be avoided by people with diabetes and kidney disease because they contain too much potassium. **SIX** Choose unsalted nuts or wipe excess salt off salted nuts with kitchen paper towels before using them in cooking. **SEVEN** Don't automatically add salt to a dish before you have tasted it to see if it needs extra flavoring.

Equipment

Having the right equipment will make it much easier for you to cook succulent and authentic Chinese meals, and Chinese supermarkets are a great place to stock up on reasonably priced equipment. Ideally, you should have the following.

NONSTICK SAUTE PAN This is ideal for stir-frying and should preferably be at least 12 inches in diameter. I prefer this type of pan to a wok when low-fat cooking because the temperature from an electric stove top or gas ring often isn't high enough to properly heat the sides of the wok. This means that it takes much longer than it should to stir-fry your food because it is competing for a small amount of cooking space at the bottom of the wok.

NONSTICK GRIDDLE PAN This is useful for cooking meats and fish and will allow you to use a minimal amount of oil.

NONSTICK SPATULA OR WOODEN SPOON Perfect for both stir-frying and mixing.

PAIR OF LONG WOODEN CHOPSTICKS These are very versatile and can be used for mixing, stir-frying, or serving food.

WOK WITH A LID AND WOK RACK FOR STEAMING A large wok is best—preferably at least 12 inches in diameter.

BAMBOO STEAMERS These should have a diameter of at least 10 inches—smaller ones look lovely but aren't very practical if you're cooking for a family. Steamers are ideal for cooking dumplings and buns, but you'll need to line the bottom with wax paper to prevent the food from sticking.

LIDDED SAUCEPANS These can be used for cooking rice or stock.

STAINLESS STEEL KNIVES OR A CLEAVER Used for chopping and cutting meat and vegetables.

CHINA CHINESE RICE BOWLS, CHOPSTICKS, AND CHINESE SPOONS Chinese eating is a social affair with the diners helping themselves to food from communal dishes in the center of the table. Go for authenticity—you can't truly enjoy Chinese food if you eat it with a knife and fork off your own plate!

Store-cupboard ingredients

The recipes in this book are simple to follow and almost always use ingredients that are widely available from good supermarkets. If you keep some of the store-cupboard essentials that are listed below, you will find it quick and easy to prepare delicious Chinese meals at home.

RICE OR FAAN This is a staple food in southern China and forms the basis of most meals. For **long grain** choose Thai Jasmine rice or brown rice. For **short grain** use either glutinous rice or Japanese sushi rice.

NOODLES These can be bought fresh or dried. **Fun** noodles are made from rice flour—for example, rice noodles. **Mein** noodles are made from wheat flour with or without the addition of egg, buckwheat, or shrimp—for example, wholewheat noodles, egg noodles, or soba (Japanese buckwheat) noodles. (Cellophane or bean thread noodles aren't actually made from rice or wheat flours but from mung beans. For this reason they tend not to be used as a staple, as they are less nutritious.)

OILS Traditionally peanut oil is used in Chinese cooking, but this has a high saturated fat content. Olive and canola oils contain less saturated fat and a higher proportion of "good" fats. Both types of oil are promoted in diets for healthy hearts because they

contain a higher proportion of monounsaturated fats, which have been shown in some scientific studies to help lower blood cholesterol. In addition, canola oil has a higher proportion of omega-3 essential fats, which are believed to help to reduce the risk of heart disease. Sesame oil, which is made from roasted white sesame seeds, is often used in Chinese cooking.

CANNED FRUITS AND VEGETABLES Canned fruits and vegetables, such as mango, lychees, bamboo shoots, and water chestnuts, are versatile and easy to use for quick meals and snacks.

LOW-FAT ALTERNATIVES Low-fat or reduced-fat coconut milk and peanut butter are now available in most large supermarkets and food stores and they usually contain at least 25 percent less fat than the original versions. They are ideal for people who want to reduce the amount of fat in their diet without sacrificing taste and flavor.

DRIED CHINESE MUSHROOMS These are relatively expensive, but a little goes a long way because they swell up once they've been reconstituted.

CORNSTARCH This is made from the starch of corn and is often used as a thickener. Some people prefer to use potato flour as a thickening agent.

TOFU OR BEAN CURD These can either be bought fresh from Oriental supermarkets or in long-life packs. They are available in two types: soft and firm. Firm is best for stir-frying, braising, and roasting; the soft variety tends to be used for making sweet desserts, drinks, and dressings.

HERBS AND SPICES Chili, garlic, ginger, scallions, cilantro, shallots, lemon grass, Thai basil leaves, five-spice powder, whole Szechwan peppercorns, peppercorns, star anise, sesame seeds, fennel seeds, ground cumin, bay leaves, cinnamon sticks, kaffir lime leaves, and tamarind paste are ideal for enhancing the taste of foods in marinades or in stir-fries so that you don't need to add extra salt.

BOTTLED SAUCES Oyster sauce, hoisin sauce, black bean sauce, and yellow bean sauce are useful for imparting distinct Chinese flavors to a dish. Sesame paste is often used to liven up cold dishes. Shoyu is a Japanese soy sauce, which contains less sodium (salt) than Chinese soy sauce. Tamari sauce is also a Japanese soy sauce that is less salty than the Chinese variety and has a richer, sweeter taste. Japanese soy sauces are brewed for longer and are made from roasted soy beans, wheat and salt. Fish sauce is made from fermented salted anchovies or from shrimp. It is an acquired taste and tends to be very salty and so should be used in only very small quantities.

VINEGAR Balsamic, rice wine, or red vinegar gives food an extra pungency. Chinese red vinegar is less acidic and is often used as a dip. Alternatively, you can dilute balsamic vinegar with equal quantities of stock or water to make a dip.

WRAPPERS Dried rice paper sheets are a useful store-cupboard ingredient. Wonton skins can be bought fresh and kept in the refrigerator for about five days or you can freeze them for later use (they are best frozen on the same day you buy them).

CHINESE RICE WINE Rice wine (preferably Shaohsing) is often used as a marinade or cooking ingredient in stir-fries. Dry sherry is an acceptable alternative.

BEANS, LENTILS, NUTS, AND SEEDS Dried, frozen, or canned pulses and beans make excellent protein alternatives to meat, as do nuts and seeds. They are all useful for livening up plain rice, noodles, or salads.

FRESH FRUIT AND VEGETABLES Popular vegetables include bok choy (pak choi), Chinese leaves, Chinese flowering cabbage (choy sum), Chinese mustard greens (kai lan), bean sprouts, Chinese flowering chives, and baby corn. Fruits include mango, lychees, star fruit (carambola), kumquats, kiwi fruit, bananas, Chinese lantern (physalis), and papaya.

Menu plans

FAMILY MENU FOR 4–6 PEOPLE

Beef and tomato *(see page 49)*

Sesame salmon with shredded vegetables *(see page 78)*

Bamboo shoots and straw mushrooms with broccoli *(see page 123)*

Vegetable chop suey *(see page 122)*

Boiled rice *(see page 140)*

Platter of oranges

FAMILY VEGETARIAN MENU FOR 4–6 PEOPLE

Fu yung with vegetables *(see page 119)*

Lentils with lemon grass and lime leaves *(see page 116)*

Stir-fried tofu with assorted vegetables *(see page 115)*

Sesame broccoli *(see page 111)*

Boiled rice *(see page 140)*

Sliced melon

TAKEOUT MENU A FOR 4–6 PEOPLE

Chicken and creamed corn soup *(see page 34)*

Beef with yellow bell peppers in black bean sauce *(see page 46)*

Sweet and sour pork *(see page 53)*

Vegetable chop suey *(see page 122)*

Vegetarian fried rice *(see page 138)*

Sesame bananas *(see page 154)*

TAKEOUT MENU B FOR 4–6 PEOPLE

Hot and sour soup *(see page 35)*

Pan-seared king shrimp with ginger and scallions *(see page 82)*

Spareribs *(see page 54)*

Chicken and cashew nuts with vegetables *(see page 70)*

Boiled rice *(see page 140)*

Lychees

ROMANTIC MENU FOR 2 PEOPLE

Shrimp and grapefruit salad (use ½ quantities) *(see page 32)*

Oysters and black bean sauce (use ½ quantities) *(see page 85)*

Duck and pineapple (use ½ quantities) *(see page 64)*

Chili kale (use ½ quantities) *(see page 110)*

Boiled rice (2 bowls) *(see page 140)*

Strawberries

BUFFET MENU FOR 8–10 PEOPLE

Sesame shrimp toasts *(see page 30)*

Fresh spring rolls *(see page 26)*

Chandoori chicken *(see page 62)*

Pork satay *(see page 57)*

Spicy fish balls with sweet and sour sauce *(see page 80)*

Sesame broccoli *(see page 111)*

Roasted tofu with Szechwan relish *(see page 106)*

Steamed buns *(see page 137)*

Almond jelly with assorted fruits *(see page 149)*

SPECIAL BANQUET MENU FOR 8–10 PEOPLE

Minty carrot and kohlrabi salad *(see page 31)*

Crispy aromatic duck *(see page 24)*

Steamed sea bass with warm scallion and ginger dressing *(see page 96)*

Garlic steamed shrimp *(see page 84)*

Roast pork *(see page 56)*

Stir-fried bok choy with shiitake mushrooms *(see page 108)*

Sea-spiced eggplants *(see page 124)*

Stir-fried noodles with peanuts and corn *(see page 130)*

Boiled rice *(see page 140)*

Tropical fruit platter *(see page 153)*

Stocks

Stocks are an important part of Chinese cooking, and making your own is the best way to impart great flavors without adding unnecessary salt, MSG, or artificial additives. Make stock in bulk, and then freeze in smaller amounts so that you always have some handy when you are cooking. It is so versatile, and can be used in soups, stews, and stir-fries.

Chicken stock

INGREDIENTS *3 pounds chicken bones* ‖ *2 pounds skinless chicken thighs and legs* ‖ *7½ pints water* ‖ *2 scallions* ‖ *2 slices fresh ginger root*

ONE Put the chicken bones into a large saucepan with the meat. **TWO** Add the water and bring to a boil. Turn down the heat to a simmer and remove any scum that rises to the top. Add the scallions and ginger, and simmer, partially covered, for 3–4 hours. **THREE** Leave the stock to cool slightly, then strain and pour into a container. Cover and store in the refrigerator until ready to use. It will keep for 2 days. Before using, skim any fat from the top of the stock.

Makes about 6½ pints

Vegetable stock

INGREDIENTS *2 pounds Chinese leaves* ‖ *2 pounds leeks* ‖ *2 pounds carrots* ‖ *2 pounds onions* ‖ *4 slices fresh ginger root* ‖ *4 bay leaves* ‖ *9½ pints water*

ONE Put the vegetables into a large saucepan with the ginger and bay leaves. **TWO** Add the water and bring to a boil. Turn down the heat to simmer, then cover the pan and simmer for 2 hours. **THREE** Leave the stock to cool slightly, then strain and pour into a container. Cover and store in the refrigerator until ready to use. It will keep for 2 days.

Makes about 5½ pints

Beef stock

INGREDIENTS *3½ pounds beef bones* ‖ *3 pounds lean braising steak, cut into pieces* ‖ *5 quarts water* ‖ *¼ pound onions, cut into chunks* ‖ *4 large carrots, cut into chunks* ‖ *3–4 slices fresh ginger root* ‖ *2 cinnamon sticks* ‖ *2 star anise*

ONE Put the beef bones and pieces into a large saucepan with the meat. **TWO** Add the water and bring it to a boil. Turn down the heat to a simmer and remove any scum that rises to the top. **THREE** Add the onions, carrots, ginger, cinnamon, and star anise, and simmer, partially covered, for 4 hours. **FOUR** Leave the stock to cool slightly, then strain and pour into a container. Cover and store in the refrigerator until ready to use. It will keep for 2 days. Before using, skim any fat from the top.

Makes about 5½ pints

Pork stock

INGREDIENTS *4 pounds pork bones* ‖ *3 pounds lean pork shoulder or leg, cut into pieces* ‖ *5 quarts water* ‖ *¼ pound onions, cut into chunks* ‖ *4 large carrots, cut into chunks* ‖ *3–4 slices fresh ginger root*

ONE Put the pork bones into a large saucepan with the meat. **TWO** Add the water and bring to a boil. Turn down the heat to simmer and remove any scum that rises to the top. Add the onions, carrots, and ginger, and simmer, partially covered, for 4 hours. **THREE** Leave the stock to cool slightly, then strain and pour into a container. Cover and store in the refrigerator until ready to use. It will keep for 2 days. Before using, skim any fat from the top.

Makes about 5½ pints

Fish stock

INGREDIENTS *1 pound fish bones* ‖ *½ pound leeks* ‖ *½ pound onions* ‖ *½ pound celery* ‖ *½ pound carrots* ‖ *5½ pints water* ‖ *handful of mixed herbs, e.g., cilantro, parsley, scallions* ‖ *2 bay leaves* ‖ *1 tablespoon white peppercorns*

ONE Wash the fish bones and put them into a large saucepan. **TWO** Peel and roughly chop the vegetables. **THREE** Add the water and bring to a boil, then turn down the heat to simmer. Remove any scum that rises to the top. Add the vegetables, herbs, and peppercorns and cook, partially covered, for 1½ hours. **FOUR** Leave the stock to cool slightly, then strain and pour into a container. Cover and store in the refrigerator for up to 24 hours until ready to use.

Makes about 3¾ pints

Lemon and fish sauce

INGREDIENTS *2 red chilies, deseeded and chopped* ‖ *½ garlic clove, crushed* ‖ *4 tablespoons fresh lemon juice* ‖ *4 tablespoons Thai fish sauce* ‖ *3 tablespoons light muscovado (unrefined) sugar* ‖ *½ cup water*

ONE Mix together all the ingredients in a bowl. **TWO** Transfer to a screw-top jar. This sauce will keep in the refrigerator for a week.

Makes about 1 cup plus 1 tablespoon

NUTRIENT ANALYSIS PER 15 ML SERVING 41 kJ – 10 cal – 0.2 g protein – 2.5 g carbohydrate – 2.0 g sugars – 0 g fat – 0 g saturated fat – 0 g fiber – 235 mg sodium

Lime and sesame dressing

INGREDIENTS *3 tablespoons toasted sesame seeds* ‖ *1 tablespoon shoyu or tamari sauce* ‖ *5 tablespoons fresh lime juice* ‖ *2 tablespoons canola or extra virgin olive oil* ‖ *1 teaspoon Worcestershire sauce*

ONE Whizz all the ingredients in a blender until thick and creamy. **TWO** Pour into a screw-top jar and store in the refrigerator until ready to use. This dressing will keep for about 1 week in the refrigerator.

Makes about 1 cup

NUTRIENT ANALYSIS PER 15 ML SERVING 58 kJ – 14 cal – 0.2 g protein – 0.1 g carbohydrate – 0.1 g sugars – 1.4 g fat – 0.2 g saturated fat – 0.1 g fiber – 19 mg sodium

Tofu and mirin dressing

INGREDIENTS *2 tablespoons mirin (Japanese rice wine)* ‖ *2 tablespoons rice vinegar* ‖ *1 tablespoon shoyu or tamari sauce* ‖ *1 tablespoon chopped fresh ginger root* ‖ *5 tablespoons silken soft tofu* ‖ *¾ cup chopped carrots*

ONE Whizz the mirin, rice vinegar, shoyu sauce, ginger, and tofu in a blender. Stir in the carrots. **TWO** This dressing can be stored in the refrigerator for a couple of days.

Makes about ¾ cup

NUTRIENT ANALYSIS PER 15 ML SERVING 27 kJ – 6 cal – 0.5 g protein – 0.6 g carbohydrate – 0.4 g sugars – 0.2 g fat – 0 g saturated fat – 0.1 g fiber – 33 mg sodium

Chili dipping sauce

INGREDIENTS *2 teaspoons cornstarch* ‖ *1 cup Vegetable Stock (see page 17)* ‖ *½ cup rice wine vinegar* ‖ *2 tablespoons shoyu or tamari sauce* ‖ *1 tablespoon soft brown sugar* ‖ *2 garlic cloves, crushed* ‖ *1 slice fresh ginger root, peeled and finely chopped* ‖ *1 red chili, deseeded and finely chopped*

ONE Combine the cornstarch and stock in a small saucepan and stir until dissolved. **TWO** Stir in the wine vinegar, shoyu sauce, sugar, garlic, ginger, and chili. Bring the sauce to a boil, stirring constantly until it has thickened. **THREE** Remove the pan from the heat and leave to cool, then spoon the sauce into a serving bowl. Use immediately.

Makes about 1¼ cups

NUTRIENT ANALYSIS PER 15 ML SERVING 23 kJ – 5.5 cal – 0.1 g protein – 1.2 g carbohydrate – 0.6 g sugars – 0 g fat – 0 g saturated fat – 0 g fiber – 34 mg sodium

Pineapple dipping sauce

INGREDIENTS *1 tablespoon rice wine vinegar* ‖ *juice of 1 lemon* ‖ *1 teaspoon brown sugar* ‖ *1 garlic clove, crushed* ‖ *2 red chilies, deseeded and sliced* ‖ *¼ pound crushed pineapple, fresh or canned in juice*

ONE Mix the vinegar, lemon juice, sugar, garlic, and chilies in a bowl. **TWO** Add the crushed pineapple and mix thoroughly. Serve immediately.

Serves 4

NUTRIENT ANALYSIS PER 15G SERVING 32 kJ – 7.3 cal – 0.1 g protein – 1.8 g carbohydrate – 1.8 g sugars – 0 g fat – 0 g saturated fat – 0.1 g fiber – trace sodium

Soups and starters

Crispy aromatic duck

This dish comes from Szechwan where, traditionally, marinated duck is steamed, then deep-fried until crisp and golden. In this recipe, the duck is also cooked first, essentially to tenderize the meat so that it comes away from the bones easily. It is then broiled rather than deep-fried to cut down the fat content.

INGREDIENTS *1 x 2-pound duck, halved and flattened slightly* ‖ *6½ pints Vegetable Stock (see page 17)*

MARINADE *1 tablespoon five-spice powder* ‖ *1 tablespoon ground ginger* ‖ *2 star anise* ‖ *2 tablespoons Szechwan peppercorns* ‖ *2 tablespoons black peppercorns* ‖ *3 tablespoons cumin seeds* ‖ *3 tablespoons fennel seeds* ‖ *1 tablespoon shoyu or tamari sauce* ‖ *6 slices fresh ginger root, peeled and crushed* ‖ *6 scallions, chopped* ‖ *2 bay leaves, crumbled*

TO SERVE *Chinese Pancakes (see page 144)* ‖ *sliced cucumber* ‖ *sliced scallions* ‖ *hoisin sauce diluted with stock*

ONE Combine the marinade ingredients and rub into the duck halves. Cover and leave overnight, or for at least a couple of hours in the refrigerator. **TWO** Bring the stock to a boil in a large saucepan. Gently lower the duck into the pan, then bring the stock back to a boil. Turn down the heat to low, cover the pan, and simmer for 45 minutes. **THREE** Leave the duck to cool in the liquid for 10–15 minutes, then remove it with a slotted spoon and pat dry on kitchen paper towels. **FOUR** Place the duck halves skin-side up on a rack set in a roasting pan. Put the pan under a preheated very hot broiler and broil for about 3–5 minutes to brown the skin. Watch closely. **FIVE** Remove the duck and blot the excess fat from the skin. Leave the duck to cool slightly, then flake the meat with 2 forks. **SIX** Serve with Chinese pancakes, sliced cucumber, sliced scallions, and some hoisin sauce diluted with a little stock.

Serves 8 as a starter

NUTRIENT ANALYSIS PER SERVING 1750 kJ – 423 cal – 20.0 g protein – 0 g carbohydrate – 0 g sugars – 38.1 g fat – 11.4 g saturated fat – 0 g fiber – 129 mg sodium

HEALTHY TIP Duck skin is high in fat, but this recipe wouldn't be what it is if the skin were removed. Some fat will be lost as part of the simmering process, yet more can be removed by blotting the duck with kitchen paper towels after broiling.

Fresh spring rolls

Deep-fried spring rolls are a firm favorite at Chinese restaurants and takeouts. This version is adapted from a Vietnamese recipe and uses soft rice paper sheets stuffed with fresh herbs and crunchy vegetables and dipped in a tasty lemony sauce.

INGREDIENTS *8 x 8½-inch round dried rice paper sheets* ‖ *Lemon and Fish Sauce (see page 19), for dipping*

FILLING *6 Chinese dried mushrooms* ‖ *2 ounces thin rice noodles* ‖ *½ pound fresh bean sprouts* ‖ *1 small cucumber, cut into strips* ‖ *2 tablespoons roughly torn fresh mint leaves* ‖ *2 tablespoons roughly torn fresh cilantro leaves* ‖ *1 carrot, grated* ‖ *2 tablespoons roasted unsalted peanuts, coarsely chopped*

ONE Put the dried mushrooms in a heatproof bowl. Cover with boiling water and put a plate on top to keep the steam in. Set aside for 20–30 minutes, or until soft. Drain the mushrooms, discard the stalks, and squeeze the water from the caps, then shred them finely. **TWO** Place the rice noodles in a bowl, pour over some boiling water, and leave to stand, covered, for about 10 minutes. Drain the noodles, rinse with cold water, and set aside. **THREE** Soak the sheets of rice paper in a bowl of warm water, one at a time, for about 30–60 seconds until softened, then place on a clean, dry dish towel. **FOUR** To prepare the spring rolls, put a little of all the filling ingredients on each rice paper sheet; roll up the bottom half of the rice paper, fold in the sides, and roll over to enclose the filling. **FIVE** The spring rolls can be prepared about 20–30 minutes before serving. Cover them with plastic wrap and place in the refrigerator until required. Serve the spring rolls with the Lemon and Fish Sauce.

Makes 8, serves 4 as a starter

NUTRIENT ANALYSIS PER ROLL 290 kJ – 70 cal – 2.7 g protein – 8.8 g carbohydrate – 1.4 g sugars – 2.7 g fat – 0.5 g saturated fat – 0.8 g fiber – 45 mg sodium

HEALTHY TIP You can use a wide variety of different colored vegetables as fillings for these spring rolls. Not only will they look attractive and appetizing, but they will also ensure that you meet your daily requirements for a wide range of phyto-nutrients.

Pan-fried dumplings

Also known as potstickers, these dumplings are popular among people from the north of China who sometimes eat them as a main meal. Here they are pan-fried but they can also be boiled or steamed.

INGREDIENTS *2½ cups strong bread flour* ‖ *1 cup hot water* ‖ *1 tablespoon canola oil* ‖ *½ cup water*

FILLING *1 cup zucchini, thinly shredded* ‖ *1¾ cups ground chicken* ‖ *1 scallion, thinly sliced* ‖ *1 tablespoon finely ground fresh ginger root* ‖ *1 teaspoon Chinese rice wine or dry sherry* ‖ *½ teaspoon freshly ground black pepper* ‖ *2 tablespoons shoyu or tamari sauce*

ONE Prepare the dough. Sift the flour into a mixing bowl. Slowly add the water to form a ball, then knead for a couple of minutes until the dough is smooth. Cover the bowl with a damp towel or plastic wrap and leave at room temperature for about 30 minutes. **TWO** Mix together all the ingredients for the filling. **THREE** Working on a lightly floured surface, roll the dough into a long cylinder about ¾ inch in diameter and cut it into about 18 pieces each ½ inch long. Cover the dough with plastic wrap to stop it drying out and use a narrow rolling pin to roll out each piece into a circle about 3 inches in diameter. The center should be slightly thicker than the edge. **FOUR** Place a heaped teaspoon of filling in the center of each wrapper and pinch tightly to seal the edges, so that it looks like an apple turnover. **FIVE** Heat a large lidded nonstick sauté pan until hot. Add the oil and swirl to cover the bottom of the pan. Lower the heat to medium and add the dumplings, making sure that there is a slight gap between each one. Turn the heat up to high; then add the water, cover with the lid, and cook for about 10 minutes, or until the water has almost evaporated. Remove the lid and cook for another couple of minutes until the bottom of the dumplings have turned golden brown. Serve the dumplings brown side up.

Makes about 18 dumplings

NUTRIENT ANALYSIS PER DUMPLING 284 kJ – 67 cal – 4.5 g protein – 10.8 g carbohydrate – 0.3 g sugars – 1.0 g fat – 0.2 g saturated fat – 0.5 g fiber – 63 mg sodium

HEALTHY TIP Zucchini are low in calories and a good source of beta carotene. They also contain some vitamin C and folate. Orange-fleshed vegetables and green leafy vegetables are important sources of vitamin A, particularly for vegans, whose diet often excludes many vitamin A-rich foods.

Lettuce wraps

Lettuce-wrapped ground chicken is a popular southern Chinese dish. This vegetarian version uses a mixture of vegetables and tofu to fill the lettuce leaves.

INGREDIENTS *6 dried Chinese mushrooms* ‖ *1 tablespoon canola or olive oil* ‖ *4 garlic cloves, crushed* ‖ *2 large shallots, sliced* ‖ *2 slices fresh ginger root, chopped* ‖ *2 fresh red chilies, deseeded and sliced* ‖ *8 canned water chestnuts, diced* ‖ *½ cup diced canned bamboo shoots* ‖ *1¼ cup diced carrots* ‖ *1 heaped tablespoon hoisin sauce* ‖ *2 teaspoons shoyu or tamari sauce* ‖ *1 x 12-ounce pack silken firm tofu, diced* ‖ *⅔ cup Vegetable Stock (see page 17)* ‖ *1½ teaspoons cornstarch* ‖ *4 scallions, sliced* ‖ *½ cup toasted walnut pieces* ‖ *freshly ground black pepper* ‖ *2 Romaine or Cos lettuces, separated into leaves*

ONE Put the dried mushrooms into a heatproof bowl, cover with boiling water, and put a plate on top to keep the steam in. Set aside for 20–30 minutes or until soft. Drain the mushrooms and remove the stalks; then squeeze the water out of the caps and chop them roughly. **TWO** Heat the oil in a nonstick pan or wok over a high heat until piping hot. Add the garlic, shallots, ginger, and chilies, and stir-fry for a couple of minutes. **THREE** Add the water chestnuts, bamboo shoots, and carrots, and stir-fry for about 5 minutes; then stir in the hoisin and shoyu sauces and season with black pepper. Add the tofu and stir gently to mix; then pour in the vegetable stock and bring to a boil. **FOUR** Meanwhile, dissolve the cornstarch in a little water in a small bowl. Push the vegetables to the sides of the wok and pour the cornstarch paste into the middle. When the sauce starts to thicken, bring in the surrounding mixture and mix well. **FIVE** Toss in the scallions and walnuts. **SIX** To serve, take a lettuce leaf, spoon on some of the tofu vegetable mixture and fold it up into a neat package to eat.

Serves 4–6 as a starter

NUTRIENT ANALYSIS PER WRAP 1064 kJ – 250 cal – 12.0 g protein – 17.2 g carbohydrate – 8.1 g sugars – 15.8 g fat – 1.7 g saturated fat – 3.3 g fiber – 181 mg sodium

HEALTHY TIP Walnuts contain a useful supply of the B vitamins, thiamin, and niacin. A recent study in the USA has shown that eating about 3½ ounces walnuts instead of saturated fats and as part of a general low-fat diet can lower blood cholesterol levels. A high blood cholesterol level is linked to an increased risk of heart disease.

Sesame shrimp toasts

Sesame shrimp toasts are popular as snacks and appetizers in the West. This low-fat baked variation of the traditionally deep-fried snack is quick and easy to make and uses French bread instead of sliced white bread.

INGREDIENTS *6 ounces raw shrimp, roughly chopped* ‖ *½ garlic clove, crushed* ‖ *½ teaspoon grated fresh ginger root* ‖ *1 small egg white, lightly beaten* ‖ *1 scallion, roughly chopped* ‖ *1 teaspoon shoyu or tamari sauce* ‖ *8 x ¾-inch slices crusty French bread* ‖ *1 teaspoon canola or olive oil* ‖ *1 tablespoon toasted sesame seeds*

ONE Whizz the shrimp, garlic, ginger, egg white, scallions, and shoyu sauce to a paste in a food processor. Chill the shrimp paste in the refrigerator for at least 20 minutes. **TWO** Toast the bread on one side, then lightly brush the untoasted side with oil. **THREE** Spread the shrimp paste evenly over the toasted side of the bread and sprinkle the sesame seeds over the top. **FOUR** Place the toasts on an oven rack and cook in a preheated oven, 475°F, for about 10 minutes, or until the shrimp paste is cooked and the toasts are crisp and browned.

Serves 4 as a starter

NUTRIENT ANALYSIS PER TOAST 492 kJ – 117 cal – 7.6 g protein – 17.9 g carbohydrate – 1.1 g sugars – 2.1 g fat – 0.2 g saturated fat – 0.7 g fiber – 255 mg sodium

HEALTHY TIP Sesame seeds are an excellent source of protein. They also provide useful amounts of vitamin E, calcium, and fiber. Choose unsalted seeds if you're watching your salt intake. Although sesame seeds are high in fat, they are mostly made up of "good" unsaturated fats, which help to lower blood cholesterol.

Minty carrot and kohlrabi salad
In Cantonese cuisine pickled vegetables are always served in sweet and sour style. This combination of tastes is thought to help stimulate the appetite and makes them ideal as appetizers.

INGREDIENTS *½ pound raw carrots, thinly sliced* ‖ *5 ounces raw kohlrabi, thinly sliced* ‖ *¾ cup water* ‖ *4½ tablespoons white wine vinegar* ‖ *1 tablespoon soft brown sugar* ‖ *½ teaspoon sea salt* ‖ *2 tablespoons chopped fresh mint leaves* ‖ *2 tablespoons chopped fresh cilantro leaves*

ONE Combine all the ingredients, apart from the mint and cilantro, in a large bowl. Cover and refrigerate for about 1 hour, stirring occasionally. **TWO** To serve, drain the carrots and kohlrabi, and discard the pickling liquid. Rinse the vegetables in water. Place them in a serving bowl and toss with the mint and cilantro leaves just before serving.

Serves 4 as a starter

NUTRIENT ANALYSIS PER SERVING 161 kJ – 39 cal – 1.2 protein – 7.9 g carbohydrate – 7.3 g sugars – 0.3 g fat – 0.1 g saturated fat – 2.3 g fiber – 69 mg sodium

HEALTHY TIP Kohlrabi belongs to the brassica family, which includes cabbage, Brussels sprouts, and broccoli. Many scientific studies have shown that these vegetables contain chemicals that can protect against some forms of cancer. For example, kohlrabi contains indoles, which may help to reduce the risk of breast cancer.

Shrimp and grapefruit salad

This dish comes from Thailand, where the pomelo is a common winter fruit. It looks like a gigantic yellow grapefruit with a slightly pointed top, but the flesh is drier and crisper than grapefruit.

INGREDIENTS *¾ pound large tiger shrimp, raw or cooked, peeled and deveined* ‖ *2 large grapefruits or 1 large pomelo, peeled and segmented* ‖ *1 small red onion, thinly sliced* ‖ *1 small ripe avocado, chopped* ‖ *4 tablespoons Lemon and Fish Sauce (see page 19)* ‖ *1 tablespoon fresh cilantro leaves*

ONE Bring a saucepan of water to a boil. Add the shrimp, if raw, and cook until they are pink, which will take 1–2 minutes. Remove the shrimp with a slotted spoon and leave to cool. **TWO** Place the grapefruit segments, onion, and avocado in a serving dish. Arrange the shrimp on top and drizzle with the sauce. Toss to mix well. **THREE** Sprinkle with the cilantro leaves and serve immediately.

Serves 4 as a starter

NUTRIENT ANALYSIS PER SERVING 766 kJ – 182 cal – 19.7 g protein – 14.0 g carbohydrate – 13.2 g sugars – 5.7 g fat – 1.1 g saturated fat – 2.9 g fiber – 432 mg sodium

HEALTHY TIP Grapefruit and pomelo are excellent sources of vitamin C. The membranes contain some insoluble fiber called pectin, which helps to lower blood cholesterol levels.

Chicken and creamed corn soup

This soup comes from southern China and is extremely popular among Westerners. The creamed-style corn and canned corn kernels give it texture, and it is thickened with a minimum of cornstarch.

INGREDIENTS *3¼ pints Chicken Stock (see page 17)* ‖ *1 x 9½-ounce can creamed-style corn* ‖ *1 x 9½-ounce can corn kernels, drained* ‖ *1 cup finely shredded cooked chicken* ‖ *½ teaspoon ground white pepper* ‖ *2 beaten eggs*

CORNSTARCH PASTE *2 teaspoons cornstarch mixed with 2 tablespoons chicken stock*

ONE Bring the stock to a boil in a large saucepan. Add the creamed-style corn and corn kernels and simmer for about 5 minutes. **TWO** Add the cooked chicken to the pan, then return the soup to a boil. Season with pepper and slowly stir in the cornstarch paste. Turn off the heat. **THREE** Stirring continuously with a pair of chopsticks, slowly drizzle in the beaten eggs. Stirring with chopsticks helps form the egg into fine threads. Serve immediately.

Serves 4

NUTRIENT ANALYSIS PER SERVING 1048 kJ – 249 cal – 14.3 g protein – 38.8 g carbohydrate – 6.8 g sugars – 5.6 g fat – 1.5 g saturated fat – 1.0 g fiber – 256 mg sodium

HEALTHY TIP Canned vegetables are an economical and convenient way of increasing your intake of vegetables. A 3¼-ounce portion of canned corn counts as one serving toward the five portions a day recommended for good health.

Hot and sour soup

This soup is found in both Szechwan and Peking cuisines. The traditional recipe calls for chicken's blood, but this vegetarian version is hot and pungent without being too overpowering.

INGREDIENTS *4 dried Chinese mushrooms* ‖ *3¼ pints Vegetable Stock (see page 17)* ‖ *1 cup shredded bamboo shoots* ‖ *1 fresh red chili, deseeded and sliced* ‖ *¼ pound silken firm tofu, cubed* ‖ *1 egg, lightly beaten*

SEASONING *1 tablespoon sherry or rice wine* ‖ *1 tablespoon white wine vinegar* ‖ *1 tablespoon lime juice* ‖ *1 teaspoon muscovado (unrefined) sugar* ‖ *1 tablespoon dark soy sauce* ‖ *1 teaspoon freshly ground black pepper*

CORNSTARCH PASTE *2 tablespoons cornstarch mixed with 4 tablespoons vegetable stock*

TO SERVE *1 tablespoon chopped fresh cilantro leaves* ‖ *1 scallion, sliced*

ONE Put the dried mushrooms in a heatproof bowl, cover with boiling water, and put a plate on top to keep the steam in. Set aside for 20–30 minutes. Drain the mushrooms and remove the stalks; squeeze the water out of the caps and chop them roughly. **TWO** Bring the stock to a boil in a large saucepan. Add the Chinese mushrooms, bamboo shoots, and chili. **THREE** Stir in all the seasoning ingredients, then add the tofu and return the soup to a boil. **FOUR** Slowly stir in the cornstarch paste to thicken the soup, then bring it back to a boil again. **FIVE** Turn off the heat and stir in the beaten egg in a steady stream, stirring it round with a fork or a pair of chopsticks. **SIX** To serve, sprinkle with the cilantro leaves and scallions.

Serves 4

NUTRIENT ANALYSIS PER SERVING 1102 kJ – 262 cal – 19.9 g protein – 32.2 g carbohydrate – 2.0 g sugars – 6.2 g fat – 1.6 g saturated fat – 0.50 g fiber – 202 mg sodium

HEALTHY TIP Capsaicin is the compound in chili that gives it its heat. Studies have shown that chili may help to lower blood pressure and blood cholesterol levels, and some people find chilies help to relieve blocked sinuses.

Steamed cashew nut and vegetable dumplings

This recipe comes from Southeast Asia. It's a bit fiddly, but you'll often find that friends, family, and children will love to get involved with making it and look forward to tucking into these little snacks when they're ready.

INGREDIENTS *3 tablespoons glutinous rice flour* ‖ *2¼ cups rice flour* ‖ *3 tablespoons arrowroot* ‖ *1½ cups water* ‖ *1 tablespoon canola or olive oil*

FILLING *2 garlic cloves, crushed* ‖ *1¼ cups finely chopped bamboo shoots* ‖ *1¼ cups finely grated carrots* ‖ *1¾ cups roasted and roughly chopped unsalted cashew nuts* ‖ *2 scallions, finely chopped* ‖ *2 tablespoons chopped fresh cilantro leaves* ‖ *1 egg* ‖ *1 tablespoon cornstarch* ‖ *1 tablespoon shoyu or tamari sauce* ‖ *1 teaspoon Thai fish sauce*

ONE To make the dough, put both kinds of rice flour in a saucepan with 1 tablespoon of the arrowroot, then stir in the water and oil. Cook over a medium heat, stirring constantly, until the mixture forms a ball and leaves the side of the pan clean. **TWO** Transfer the dough to a mixing bowl and, while it's still firm, knead it for about 2–3 minutes until it is smooth and shiny. Cover with plastic wrap until ready to use. **THREE** Mix all the ingredients for the filling in a large bowl. **FOUR** With your hands, roll the dough into small balls about ½ inch in diameter; then, with a small rolling pin, roll the dough into circles about 3 inches in diameter. **FIVE** Place a heaped tablespoon of filling in the center of each wrapper. Fold over the sides to form semicircles and press the edges together. **SIX** Pour about 2 inches of water into a wok. Place a metal or wooden rack in the wok and bring the water to a boil. **SEVEN** Line the bottom of a bamboo steamer with wax paper. **EIGHT** Place 8–10 dumplings in the bamboo steamer and put it on top of the wok rack. Cover and steam for 10–12 minutes, or until the dough is cooked and translucent. Check the water levels periodically and top up with hot water if necessary. Serve with Chili Dipping Sauce *(see page 21)* or Pineapple Dipping Sauce *(see page 21)*.

Serves 8 as a starter or a light lunch

NUTRIENT ANALYSIS PER DUMPLING 1520 kJ – 364 cal – 8.3 g protein – 49.7 g carbohydrate – 2.8 g sugars – 14.5 g fat – 3.0 g saturated fat – 1.7 g fiber – 134 mg sodium

HEALTHY TIP Cilantro is used in Asian and oriental cuisine for flavoring curries, salads, and sauces. In traditional folk medicine, it is used for treating urinary tract infections.

Butternut squash and tofu soup

It's unusual in traditional Chinese cooking to find the blended soups so often seen in other parts of the world. This recipe is so wickedly creamy and delicious that you might think it contains milk or cream. Pumpkin can be substituted for the butternut squash, if you like.

INGREDIENTS *1 large onion, roughly chopped* ‖ *5 ounces carrots, cut into large chunks* ‖ *1 butternut squash, weighing about 1¼–1½ pounds, peeled and cut into large chunks* ‖ *1 slice fresh ginger root* ‖ *2½ cups Vegetable Stock (see page 17)* ‖ *½ pound silken soft tofu, roughly chopped*

ONE In a large saucepan, sweat the onion over a low heat for about 10 minutes. **TWO** Add the carrots, butternut squash, ginger, and stock; then bring the mixture to a boil over a high heat. **THREE** Reduce the heat to low and simmer for about 25–30 minutes until all the vegetables are soft. **FOUR** Add the tofu, stir and bring the soup back to a boil over a medium heat. **FIVE** Pour the mixture into a food processor or blender and blend for about 30 seconds until the soup is smooth and creamy.

Serves 4–6

NUTRIENT ANALYSIS PER SERVING 611 kJ – 145 cal – 8.0 g protein – 22.9 g carbohydrate – 14.3 g sugars – 3.1 g fat – 0.4 g saturated fat – 4.5 g fiber – 21 mg sodium

HEALTHY TIP Butternut squash is a good source of beta carotene and vitamin E, both of which act as antioxidants, protecting the body against free radicals, which can increase our risk of developing heart disease and some cancers.

Wonton soup

Wontons are small dumplings that are often served in soup either on their own or with noodles; they are a very popular street food in oriental countries. Wonton wrappers can be found in the chiller cabinet in Chinese supermarkets and can be frozen, ideally on the day they are bought.

INGREDIENTS *45 wonton wrappers* ‖ *3¼ pints Pork Stock (see page 18) or Chicken Stock (see page 17)* ‖ *8 Chinese leaves, shredded* ‖ *2 scallions, sliced*

STUFFING *1 cup ground lean pork or chicken* ‖ *1 cup roughly chopped raw shrimp* ‖ *2 scallions, finely sliced* ‖ *2 slices fresh ginger root, peeled and finely chopped* ‖ *¾ cup finely chopped bamboo shoots* ‖ *1 egg white, lightly beaten* ‖ *1 tablespoon shoyu or tamari sauce* ‖ *½ teaspoon freshly ground black pepper* ‖ *1 teaspoon Chinese rice wine or dry sherry* ‖ *1 teaspoon sesame oil* ‖ *1 teaspoon cornstarch*

ONE Mix the ingredients for the stuffing thoroughly in a large bowl. **TWO** To wrap the wontons, place about ½ teaspoon of filling in the center of each wonton wrapper. Brush 2 of the edges of the wrapper with water, fold over the wonton, and seal to make a triangle. **THREE** Bring a large pan of water to a boil. Meanwhile, heat the stock in another saucepan and add the Chinese leaves. **FOUR** Gently lower a handful of wontons into a boiling water with a slotted spoon. Stir very gently to separate the wontons and make sure that they don't stick at the bottom of the pan. **FIVE** Bring the water back to a boil and cook the wontons, uncovered, for 5–6 minutes, or until they are done and have floated to the surface. Transfer to a large serving bowl. **SIX** To serve, pour the stock and Chinese leaves over the wontons and sprinkle with the scallions.

Serves 5–6 as a starter

NUTRIENT ANALYSIS PER SERVING 389 kJ – 92 cal – 11.7 g protein – 8.0 g carbohydrate – 0.3 g sugars – 1.4 g fat – 0.4 g saturated fat – 0.2 g fiber – 203 mg sodium

HEALTHY TIP Traditionally, fatty pork is used for the wonton filling. Using lean pork or chicken makes the wontons lower in fat. Serve them with noodles and vegetables to make a complete low-fat light meal.

Tofu and mushrooms in lemon grass fragrant broth

This low-fat soup is easy to prepare and makes an excellent starter for a vegetarian meal.

INGREDIENTS *4¼ cups Vegetable Stock (see page 17)* ‖ *2 lemon grass stalks, lightly crushed* ‖ *1 red chili, chopped* ‖ *2 teaspoons shoyu or tamari sauce* ‖ *pinch of white pepper* ‖ *1¾ cups chopped closed cap mushrooms* ‖ *½ pound silken firm tofu, cubed* ‖ *juice of ½ lime* ‖ *handful of fresh basil leaves* ‖ *2 scallions, sliced lengthwise*

ONE Bring the stock to a boil in a saucepan. Add the lemon grass and red chili; then leave to simmer for about 15–20 minutes, covered. **TWO** Season the broth with shoyu sauce and pepper. **THREE** Add the mushrooms and tofu, and cook for 5–10 minutes. **FOUR** Add the lime juice, basil leaves, and scallions and stir gently. Serve immediately.

Serves 4 as an appetizer

NUTRIENT ANALYSIS PER SERVING 414 kJ – 99 cal – 12.1 g protein – 1.3 g carbohydrate – 0.5 g sugars – 4.9 g fat – 0.9 g saturated fat – 0.7 g fiber – 479 mg sodium

HEALTHY TIP Tofu or bean curd is an excellent source of the plant hormone phyto-oestrogen. Research suggests that soy and soy products such as tofu can help to protect against breast cancer and osteoporosis and may help to alleviate the symptoms of the menopause.

Meat

Pan-seared beef with garlic and chili sauce

This recipe is an adaptation of the Thai dish known as "shaking" beef, which gets its name from the sound of the pan being shaken as the beef is cooked. This dish goes well with Sticky Rice *(see page 141)* or Boiled Rice *(see page 140)* and stir-fried vegetables.

INGREDIENTS *¾ pound sirloin beef, cut into ½-inch thick slices* ‖ *1 teaspoon sesame oil*

GARLIC AND CHILI DIPPING SAUCE *2 garlic cloves, crushed* ‖ *1 tablespoon shoyu or tamari sauce* ‖ *1 teaspoon light muscovado (unrefined) sugar* ‖ *2 red chilies, deseeded and finely chopped* ‖ *1 tablespoon lime juice*

ONE Beat the beef on both sides with a meat mallet to make it slightly thinner. **TWO** Brush the beef with the sesame oil and set aside. **THREE** Mix together all the ingredients for the dipping sauce in a small bowl and set aside. **FOUR** Place the beef on a preheated, very hot griddle pan. For medium beef, cook for about 1½ minutes on each side until browned. Remove from the pan and let the beef rest for about 1 minute, then slice thinly into ½-inch strips. **FIVE** Serve the beef with the dipping sauce.

Serves 4 with 2 other main dishes

NUTRIENT ANALYSIS PER SERVING 630 kJ – 150 cal – 23.9 g protein – 1.9 g carbohydrate – 1.4 g sugars – 5.3 g fat – 2.1 g saturated fat – 0.1 g fiber – 196 mg sodium

HEALTHY TIP Beef is a valuable source of the minerals iron, zinc, manganese, selenium, and chromium. Iron is essential for healthy blood; zinc is important for normal growth and development; manganese is used for the healthy formation of bones; selenium is vital for sexual development; and chromium is needed for the regulation of blood sugar and cholesterol levels.

Shredded beef with carrots and chili

This classic dish comes from Peking, where deep-fried beef strips are stir-fried with carrot strips in a spicy sauce. In this reduced-fat recipe, the beef is also precooked but less oil is used as the beef strips are coated in cornstarch and pan-fried before stir-frying. This dish goes well with boiled rice noodles and Stir-fried Cabbage *(see page 107)*.

INGREDIENTS *¾ pound round steak, cut into thin strips, 2½ inches long* ǁ *2 tablespoons cornstarch* ǁ *1 tablespoon canola or olive oil* ǁ *2 garlic cloves, crushed* ǁ *2–3 fresh red chilies, deseeded and sliced* ǁ *¾ pound carrots, cut into thin strips, 2½ inches long* ǁ *2 teaspoons Chinese rice wine or dry sherry* ǁ *2 teaspoons rice wine vinegar* ǁ *½ tablespoon tomato ketchup* ǁ *1 teaspoon dark muscovado (unrefined) sugar* ǁ *2 teaspoons shoyu or tamari sauce* ǁ *3 scallions, sliced, to garnish*

ONE Put the beef strips in a bowl and mix in the cornstarch. **TWO** Heat the oil in a nonstick sauté pan until piping hot. Add the beef and fry for 1 minute on each side. Remove from the pan and set aside. **THREE** Add the garlic and chilies to the pan and stir-fry for a few seconds. Toss in the carrots; then add the rice wine, vinegar, ketchup, sugar, and shoyu sauce and stir-fry for 1 more minute. **FOUR** Add the beef and mix with the carrot mixture. Serve garnished with the scallion slices.

Serves 4 with 2 other main dishes

NUTRIENT ANALYSIS PER SERVING 953 kJ – 227 cal – 23.1 g protein – 16.9 g carbohydrate – 9.1 g sugars – 7.3 g fat – 2.2 g saturated fat – 2.6 g fiber – 174 mg sodium

HEALTHY TIP Carrots are even more nutritious cooked than raw. This is because the cell walls of raw carrots are tough and the cooking process helps breaks them down to make the beta carotene (the vegetable equivalent of vitamin A) easier for the body to absorb.

Beef with yellow bell peppers and black bean sauce

This version of a popular Cantonese dish is cooked with beef stock, which makes the sauce rich and tasty without needing the addition of salt or monosodium glutamate (MSG). This is an excellent dish to serve with Stir-fried Bok Choy with Shiitake Mushrooms *(see page 108)*.

INGREDIENTS *½ tablespoon olive oil* ‖ *1 tablespoon black bean sauce* ‖ *¾ pound round or filet steak, sliced* ‖ *1 red chili, deseeded and cut into strips* ‖ *3½ ounces onion, chopped in squares* ‖ *10 ounces yellow bell peppers, cored, deseeded, and chopped in squares* ‖ *¾ cup hot Beef Stock (see page 18)*

CORNSTARCH PASTE *1 teaspoon cornstarch mixed with 1 tablespoon water or stock*

ONE Heat the oil in a nonstick sauté pan over a high heat until hot. Add the black bean sauce and stir-fry for a few seconds; then add the sliced beef and stir-fry for about 1 minute until half-cooked. **TWO** Mix in the chili, onion, and yellow bell peppers, and stir-fry for about 1–2 minutes. **THREE** Add the hot stock and bring to a boil. **FOUR** Slowly stir in the cornstarch paste until the sauce has thickened and become transparent. Serve immediately.

Serves 4 with 2 other main dishes

NUTRIENT ANALYSIS PER SERVING 817 kJ – 195 cal – 23.6 g protein – 6.7 g carbohydrate – 3.7 g sugars – 8.4 g fat – 3.2 g saturated fat – 1.0 g fiber – 221 mg sodium

HEALTHY TIP Lean beef, such as filet and round steak, is an excellent source of iron, which is needed for healthy blood. Trimming excess visible fat ensures that this dish is low in fat.

Beef in oyster sauce

Beef in oyster sauce is a popular Chinese takeout dish; this recipe also includes snow peas, which give an added crunch to the juicy and succulent beef. This dish goes well with Steamed Sea Bass Fillets with Scallion and Ginger Dressing *(see page 98)*. Serve the two dishes as part of a family meal.

INGREDIENTS *¾ pound snow peas* ‖ *1 tablespoon canola or olive oil* ‖ *1 garlic clove, crushed* ‖ *1 pound filet steak, thinly sliced* ‖ *3½ tablespoons hot Beef Stock (see page 18)* ‖ *1 tablespoon oyster sauce*

CORNSTARCH PASTE *½ tablespoon cornstarch mixed with 2 tablespoons water*

ONE Blanch the snow peas in a large pan of boiling water for 30 seconds; then remove with a slotted spoon and place on a serving dish. **TWO** Heat the oil in a nonstick sauté pan over a high heat. Add the garlic and stir-fry for a few seconds until it is fragrant and beginning to brown. **THREE** Add the filet steak and cook for 1 minute on each side. **FOUR** Add the hot stock and oyster sauce, and stir to mix thoroughly. Slowly stir in the cornstarch paste and cook until the sauce has thickened. **FIVE** Pour the beef mixture over the snow peas and serve immediately.

Serves 4 with 2 other main dishes

NUTRIENT ANALYSIS PER SERVING 902 kJ – 215 cal – 28.6 g protein – 8.4 g carbohydrate – 3.4 g sugar – 7.6 g fat – 2.3 g saturated fat – 2.3 g fiber – 228 mg sodium

HEALTHY TIP Snow peas are an excellent source of vitamin C. They can be eaten raw in salads as well as stir-fried in oriental dishes.

Beef and tomato

This dish is a popular item on the menu of most Chinese takeouts. It is important to choose a lean, good quality beef; otherwise you will end up with an inedible dish. The dish goes well with Vegetable Chop Suey *(see page 122)*.

INGREDIENTS *1 teaspoon shoyu or tamari sauce* ‖ *2 teaspoons cornstarch* ‖ *2 teaspoons Chinese rice wine or dry sherry* ‖ *1 pound round steak, thinly sliced* ‖ *1 tablespoon canola or olive oil* ‖ *2 garlic cloves, sliced* ‖ *2 slices fresh ginger root, peeled and finely chopped* ‖ *1 pound fresh tomatoes, preferably plum tomatoes* ‖ *3½ tablespoons Beef Stock* (see page 18)

CORNSTARCH PASTE *1 teaspoon cornstarch mixed with 1 tablespoon water*

ONE Mix together the shoyu sauce, cornstarch, and rice wine, and rub into the sliced beef. Set aside to marinate for 10 minutes. **TWO** Heat the oil in a nonstick sauté pan over a high heat until hot. Add the garlic and ginger, and stir-fry for a few seconds. **THREE** Add the beef slices and stir-fry for 1 minute on each side. Remove and set aside. **FOUR** In the same pan, add the fresh tomatoes and cook over a medium heat for 1 minute; then add the beef stock. Turn the heat to low, cover the pan, and simmer for 5 minutes. **FIVE** Return the beef slices to the pan and mix thoroughly; then add the cornstarch paste, stirring continuously until the sauce has thickened and turned transparent.

Serves 4 with 2 other main dishes

NUTRIENT ANALYSIS PER SERVING 896 kJ – 213 cal – 25.8 g protein – 9.9 g carbohydrate – 3.6 g sugar – 7.8 g fat – 2.4 g saturated fat – 1.2 g fiber – 123 mg sodium

HEALTHY TIP Tomatoes are a good source of lycopene, a pigment that makes the tomato red. Research has found that lycopene may help to prevent certain forms of cancer, such as prostate cancer. Cooking the tomatoes makes the lycopene easier for the body to absorb.

Spiced beef and vegetable stew

This recipe originates from Vietnam. Don't expect a thick stew from this recipe—it's more like a *pot au feu*. This dish goes well with steamed yam (steam peeled slices of yam over a high heat for 20 minutes) and Sesame Broccoli *(see page 111)*.

INGREDIENTS *1 tablespoon canola or olive oil* ‖ *1 large onion, chopped* ‖ *4 slices fresh ginger root, peeled and roughly chopped* ‖ *2 fresh chilies, deseeded and sliced* ‖ *1 pound lean braising or stewing steak, cut into 1-inch cubes* ‖ *2 garlic cloves, crushed* ‖ *2½ cups Beef Stock (see page 18)* ‖ *5 star anise* ‖ *1 teaspoon five-spice powder* ‖ *1 cinnamon stick* ‖ *1 teaspoon fennel seeds* ‖ *2 dried kaffir lime leaves* ‖ *1 lemon grass stalk, chopped* ‖ *1 teaspoon black peppercorns* ‖ *2 tablespoons shoyu or tamari sauce* ‖ *¾ pound carrots, cut into ½-inch slices* ‖ *1 pound mooli or turnips, cut into ½-inch slices* ‖ *fresh chives, to garnish*

ONE Heat the oil in a nonstick sauté pan or wok over a high heat until hot. **TWO** Add the onion, ginger, and chilies. Stir and cook over a medium heat for about 5–7 minutes. **THREE** Turn up the heat to high. Add the beef and fry for about 5–10 minutes until lightly browned, stirring occasionally. **FOUR** Add the garlic, stock, star anise, five-spice powder, cinnamon, fennel seeds, lime leaves, lemon grass, peppercorns, and shoyu sauce. Stir and bring the mixture back to a boil; then turn down the heat to a simmer. Cover the pan and cook over a low heat for 1½ hours, stirring occasionally. Add the carrots and mooli, and continue cooking, covered, for another 45 minutes, or until the vegetables have softened. **FIVE** To serve, skim any fat off the surface and garnish with the chopped chives.

Serves 4 as a main dish

NUTRIENT ANALYSIS PER SERVING 1183 kJ – 283 cal – 30.5 g protein – 17.8 g carbohydrate – 14.6 g sugars – 10.7 g fat – 3.5 g saturated fat – 3.4 g fiber – 393 mg sodium

HEALTHY TIP Stews and casseroles lend themselves very well to the addition of a variety of root vegetables, such as the carrots and mooli in this recipe. They can be included as a portion of the five-a-day needed for good health.

Steamed pork balls with plum relish

This is a variation of a Chinese regional Hakka dish from southern China, a very wholesome style of cooking. This dish goes very well with Sticky Rice *(see page 141)* and Sesame Broccoli *(see page 111)*.

INGREDIENTS *1 pound lean ground pork* ‖ *2 teaspoons shoyu or tamari sauce* ‖ *1 teaspoon sesame oil* ‖ *1 small shallot, finely chopped* ‖ *1 egg, lightly beaten* ‖ *1 tablespoon cornstarch* ‖ *1 tablespoon fresh cilantro leaves, to garnish*

PLUM RELISH *1 star anise, crushed* ‖ *½ teaspoon freshly grated orange rind* ‖ *2 large shallots, chopped* ‖ *1 tablespoon finely grated fresh ginger root* ‖ *2 tablespoons Vegetable Stock (see page 17)* ‖ *1 tablespoon plum sauce* ‖ *1 pound fresh red plums, pitted and quartered*

ONE Mix together the pork, shoyu or tamari sauce, sesame oil, shallot, egg, and cornstarch in a large bowl. Cover and set aside in the refrigerator for about 20 minutes. **TWO** Meanwhile, make the plum relish. Simmer the star anise, orange rind, shallots, ginger, stock, plum sauce, and plums over a low heat for about 15 minutes, or until the plums are soft. Remove from the heat and set aside to cool. **THREE** Pour about 2 inches of water into a wok. Place a metal or wooden rack in the wok and bring the water to a boil. **FOUR** Make the pork balls. Take a tablespoon of the pork mixture and roll it into a ball. Repeat until all the mixture has been used. **FIVE** Put the pork balls in a heatproof bowl and set it on the rack. Cover the wok and steam the pork balls over a high heat for 10–12 minutes, or until done. Check the water level from time to time and top up with hot water if necessary. **SIX** Serve the pork balls in a bowl with the plum sauce and sprinkle with the cilantro leaves.

Serves 4 with 2 other dishes

NUTRIENT ANALYSIS PER SERVING 1124 kJ – 266 cal – 30.7 g protein – 19.9 g carbohydrate – 12.6 g sugars – 7.8 g fat – 2.4 g saturated fat – 2.4 g fiber – 194 mg sodium

HEALTHY TIP Plums are a good source of vitamin E, which acts as an antioxidant, helping to protect cells from damage by free radicals and which can help to reduce some of the signs of aging.

Sweet and sour pork

This is a Cantonese dish, which is extremely popular in Chinese takeouts and restaurants. However, this recipe uses lean pork rather than the traditional belly pork. Recreate your own takeout menu by serving this with Vegetable Chop Suey *(see page 123)* and Vegetarian Fried Rice *(see page 138)*.

INGREDIENTS *1 egg white, slightly beaten ‖ 1 teaspoon freshly ground black pepper ‖ 1 pound pork tenderloin or loin, cut into ½-inch thick slices ‖ 4 tablespoons cornstarch ‖ 1 tablespoon canola or olive oil*

SWEET AND SOUR SAUCE *3 tablespoons tomato ketchup ‖ 1 teaspoon white wine vinegar ‖ 7 ounces fresh tomatoes, roughly chopped ‖ 4 tablespoons pineapple juice ‖ 2 teaspoons sugar ‖ ¾ cup water ‖ 5 ounces pineapple pieces ‖ 5 ounces green bell pepper, cored, deseeded and cut into 1-inch squares ‖ ¼ pound onion, cut into 1-inch squares ‖ juice of 1 lemon*

CORNSTARCH PASTE *5 teaspoons cornstarch mixed with 5 tablespoons stock or water*

ONE Mix the egg white and pepper and rub into the pork slices. Dip each piece of pork into the cornstarch, shaking off the excess. **TWO** Heat the oil in a nonstick sauté pan over a high heat until piping hot. **THREE** Put the pork slices into the sauté pan, making sure there is a little space between each one, and fry for 2 minutes on each side. Turn down the heat to medium and stir-fry the pork for another 2 minutes, or until done. Transfer to a serving plate and keep warm. **FOUR** Make the sweet and sour sauce. Combine all the ingredients in a small saucepan. Bring to a boil, and thicken with the cornstarch paste. **FIVE** Pour the sauce over the pork and serve.

Serves 4 with 2 other main dishes

NUTRIENT ANALYSIS PER SERVING 1570 kJ – 372 cal – 26.9 g protein – 44.9 g carbohydrate – 9.7 g sugar – 10.7 g fat – 3.1 g saturated fat – 1.6 g fiber – 249 mg sodium

HEALTHY TIP Bell peppers are an excellent source of vitamin C and beta carotene, both of which act as antioxidants, helping to mop up damaging free radicals. Vitamin C is also needed for healthy skin and promoting immune function.

Spareribs

Spareribs are a popular Chinese dish. This particular recipe has been adapted from one that was a bestseller in my parents-in-law's takeout. Serve with Steamed Buns *(see page 137)* and Lettuce Wraps *(see page 28)* for an unusual Sunday lunch.

INGREDIENTS *2 pounds lean pork spareribs* ‖ *2½ pints hot Vegetable Stock (see page 17) or a Meat Stock (see pages 17 and 18)*

MARINADE *1 teaspoon five-spice powder* ‖ *2 star anise* ‖ *1 tablespoon Szechwan peppercorns* ‖ *1 tablespoon black peppercorns* ‖ *2 large shallots, chopped* ‖ *1 heaped tablespoon hoisin sauce* ‖ *1 tablespoon shoyu or tamari sauce* ‖ *6 slices fresh ginger root, peeled and crushed* ‖ *6 scallions, chopped* ‖ *2 bay leaves, crumbled* ‖ *1 orange, cut into wedges*

CORNSTARCH PASTE (OPTIONAL) *4 teaspoons cornstarch mixed with 4 tablespoons water*

ONE Mix together all the marinade ingredients and rub into the spareribs. Put them in a shallow dish and marinate in the refrigerator for at least a couple of hours and preferably overnight. **TWO** Line a roasting pan with a large piece of foil. Put the spareribs and marinade into the pan and pour over the hot stock. Cook for 1 hour in a preheated oven, 475°F, then turn the ribs over. **THREE** Reduce the heat to 350°F, and cook for another 45 minutes, or until the ribs are browned and soft. **FOUR** Remove the ribs with a slotted spoon and place on a serving plate. Pour the remaining sauce from the bottom of the roasting pan into a small saucepan and thicken with some cornstarch paste, if you like, stirring until the sauce has thickened and turned transparent.

Serves 4

NUTRIENT ANALYSIS PER SERVING 1993 kJ – 275 cal – 62.7 g protein – 10.9 g carbohydrate – 6.7 g sugars – 20.5 g fat – 7.2 g saturated fat – 1.5 g fiber – 297 mg sodium

HEALTHY TIP Spareribs can be high in fat, particularly if they are deep-fried. Removing any excess visible fat before and after cooking will help reduce the fat content.

Roast pork

This is my version of Char Siu, but don't expect to see the ubiquitous red color you might be familiar with in restaurants and takeouts. Using vinegar in the marinade makes the surface of the pork turn temptingly brown when it's been roasted. The Szechwan peppercorns give the dish an aromatic, citrus flavor without being overpowering. Serve with Vegetarian Fried Rice *(see page 138)*.

INGREDIENTS *1 pound boneless and skinless pork loin* ‖ *2 tablespoons Chinese red wine vinegar or balsamic vinegar* ‖ *1 tablespoon fennel seeds* ‖ *½ tablespoon olive oil* ‖ *1 tablespoon crushed Szechwan peppercorns*

ONE Put the pork in a roasting pan with the vinegar, fennel seeds, and olive oil. Sprinkle with the peppercorns (don't touch them with your bare hands because they can irritate in the same way as chilies) and set aside to marinate for 30 minutes. **TWO** Cook the pork in a preheated oven, 425°F, for 40 minutes, or until cooked. **THREE** Remove the pork from the oven and leave to cool for 20 minutes in the pan; then slice thinly. Drizzle some gravy from the pan over the meat.

Serves 4 with 2 other main dishes

NUTRIENT ANALYSIS PER SERVING 754 kJ – 181 cal – 25.2 g protein – trace carbohydrates – trace sugars – 9.2 g fat – 2.8 g saturated fat – 0 g fiber – 62 mg sodium

HEALTHY TIP Pork is an excellent source of energy, providing B vitamins and zinc, which are needed to maintain a healthy immune system.

Pork satay

This popular Southeast Asian dish is ideal for barbecues. The satay sauce can be prepared beforehand, and you can use other meats, such as chicken, beef, or lamb, or even shrimp instead of the pork. Serve with thick cucumber slices and Sticky Rice *(see page 141)*.

INGREDIENTS *1 teaspoon ground turmeric* ‖ *1 teaspoon ground coriander* ‖ *1 teaspoon ground cumin* ‖ *1 tablespoon lime juice* ‖ *1 tablespoon shoyu or tamari sauce* ‖ *1 teaspoon sesame oil* ‖ *1 pound pork tenderloin, cut into ¼-inch x ½-inch pieces*

SATAY SAUCE *1 cup light coconut milk* ‖ *¼ cup reduced-fat peanut butter* ‖ *2 teaspoons red curry paste* ‖ *½ teaspoon lime juice*

ONE Soak some wooden satay sticks in water for 15–20 minutes. **TWO** Mix the turmeric, coriander, cumin, lime juice, and shoyu sauce, and rub into the pork tenderloin. Cover and chill for at least 1 hour. **THREE** Mix all the sauce ingredients in a small saucepan and simmer for 20 minutes, stirring occasionally to prevent the sauce sticking to the pan. Transfer to a small bowl and leave to cool. **FOUR** Thread 3–4 pork cubes onto each satay stick. **FIVE** Place the satay sticks on a roasting rack under a preheated, very hot broiler and cook for 10–12 minutes, or until done, turning them frequently to prevent burning.

Serves 4 as a light meal

NUTRIENT ANALYSIS PER SERVING, INCLUDING THE SAUCE 915 kJ – 278 cal – 28.1 g protein – 6.4 g carbohydrate – 4.5 g sugars – 15.4 g fat – 6.2 g saturated fat – 1.5 g fiber – 192 mg sodium

HEALTHY TIP Satay sauce can be very high in fat. This recipe uses reduced-fat coconut milk and peanut butter, which both contain 25 percent less fat than the standard versions.

Poultry

Chicken with lemon grass and asparagus

This dish has a Thai influence, with lots of lemon grass, ginger, and basil leaves. The addition of vine-ripened tomatoes moistens it and lends a taste of the Mediterranean. Serve with Shrimp and Grapefruit Salad *(see page 32)* as a starter.

INGREDIENTS *1 tablespoon canola or olive oil* ‖ *2 garlic cloves, crushed* ‖ *2 tablespoons finely chopped lemon grass* ‖ *2 teaspoons finely chopped fresh ginger root* ‖ *1 onion, sliced* ‖ *1 pound chicken breast, cut into strips* ‖ *10 ounces vine-ripened tomatoes, chopped* ‖ *¾ pound asparagus stalks, halved length- and widthwise* ‖ *1 tablespoon shoyu or tamari sauce* ‖ *½ teaspoon ground black pepper* ‖ *handful of Thai basil leaves, to garnish*

ONE Heat the oil in a nonstick sauté pan over a high heat until hot, swirling it around the pan. **TWO** Toss in the garlic, lemon grass, ginger, and onion, and stir-fry for about 5 minutes. **THREE** Add the chicken and stir-fry for about 5–7 minutes until the chicken is browned and cooked. **FOUR** Add the tomatoes, asparagus, shoyu sauce, and pepper, and stir-fry for about 2–3 minutes to warm through. Garnish with the Thai basil leaves.

Serves 4

NUTRIENT ANALYSIS PER SERVING 825 kJ – 196 cal – 30.9 g protein – 7.7 g carbohydrate – 6.2 g sugars – 4.8 g fat – 0.9 g saturated fat – 2.9 g fiber – 202 mg sodium

HEALTHY TIP Asparagus is best eaten on the day it's bought, since it loses its freshness rapidly when stored. In folk medicine, it is used as a tonic to treat various ills, including rheumatism and toothache.

Chandoori chicken

This is my Chinese version of tandoori chicken, flavored with an oriental mix of spices and roasted in the oven. It can also be cooked on a barbecue. This dish is best served as finger food with cucumber sticks and roasted sweet potato slices and a Tofu and Mirin Dressing *(see page 20)* or a Chili Dipping Sauce *(see page 21)*.

INGREDIENTS *4 x 3½-ounce boneless, skinless chicken thighs* ‖ *1 lime, cut into wedges*

MARINADE *1 star anise* ‖ *1 teaspoon Szechwan peppercorns* ‖ *1 teaspoon black peppercorns* ‖ *1 lemon grass stalk, finely chopped* ‖ *2 garlic cloves, crushed* ‖ *1 teaspoon finely chopped fresh ginger root* ‖ *1 tablespoon shoyu or tamari sauce* ‖ *1 teaspoon sesame oil* ‖ *1 teaspoon five-spice powder*

ONE Make the marinade. Coarsely pound the star anise, Szechwan and black peppercorns, lemon grass, garlic, and ginger to a paste in a mortar. Mix in the shoyu sauce, sesame oil, and five-spice powder until well blended. **TWO** Put the chicken thighs in a bowl and rub with the marinade. Cover and chill for at least 1 hour. **THREE** Transfer the chicken thighs to a rack and cook in a preheated oven, 475°F, for 20 minutes, or until done.

Serves 4 with a side dish as a light lunch or supper

NUTRIENT ANALYSIS PER SERVING 504 kJ – 120 cal – 21.5 g protein – 0.7 g carbohydrate – 0.1 g sugars – 3.7 g fat – 0.9 g saturated fat – 0.1 g fiber – 21 mg sodium

HEALTHY TIP Chicken is naturally low in fat. Broiling instead of frying in oil is a great way of serving a delicious light meal for those who are watching their waistlines.

Duck and pineapple

This is another classic Chinese dish which is found on the menus of most Chinese takeouts and restaurants. The sharpness from the pineapple complements the richness of the duck perfectly.

INGREDIENTS *2 x 3½-ounce duck breasts, skin removed* ‖ *½ teaspoon sesame oil* ‖ *½ teaspoon freshly ground black pepper* ‖ *½ pound pineapple chunks, canned in juice* ‖ *2 slices fresh ginger root* ‖ *1 tablespoon shoyu or tamari sauce*

CORNSTARCH PASTE *1 teaspoon cornstarch mixed with 2 tablespoons water*

ONE Rub the duck breasts with the sesame oil and black pepper and set aside. **TWO** Heat a griddle pan over a high heat until piping hot. Add the duck breasts and cook for 2–3 minutes on each side for medium done. Remove and blot any excess oil on kitchen paper towels. **THREE** To make the sauce, pour the pineapple chunks and their juice into a pan. Add the ginger slices and cook over a medium heat for about 3–4 minutes. Stir in the shoyu sauce and bring the mixture to a boil. Slowly stir in the cornstarch paste, a little at a time, to thicken the sauce. **FOUR** To serve, pour the sauce onto a serving plate. Slice the duck breasts and arrange them on the sauce. This dish goes very well with a mixture of jasmine and wild rice.

Serves 4 with 2 other dishes

NUTRIENT ANALYSIS PER SERVING 1007 kJ – 240 cal – 23.9 g protein – 14.3 g carbohydrate – 6.9 g sugars – 10.1 g fat – 3.1 g saturated fat – 0.3 g fiber – 219 mg sodium

HEALTHY TIP Duck is a fatty bird, particularly if you eat the skin as well. A typical 3½-ounce serving of duck meat and skin will supply about 1¼ ounces fat, while the fat content of duck meat only is ⅓ ounce. Duck is a good source of the B vitamins thiamine and riboflavin, and contains more iron than chicken.

Chicken chop suey

Chop suey literally means assorted bits. This recipe comes from my husband, who used to make large quantities every Saturday night when he was working in his parents' takeout. He can almost cook it with his eyes closed! Dishes with robust seasonings, such as Beef and Tomato *(see page 49)* and Sea-spiced Eggplants *(see page 124),* go well with this.

INGREDIENTS *½ teaspoon canola or olive oil ‖ 1 teaspoon sesame oil ‖ 1 large shallot, finely chopped ‖ 1 garlic clove, crushed ‖ 7 ounces chicken breast, sliced into strips ‖ ¾ pound fresh bean sprouts ‖ 2 ounces canned sliced bamboo shoots, drained ‖ 3½ ounces canned tomatoes, drained and crushed ‖ 2 teaspoons shoyu or tamari sauce ‖ 2 scallions, chopped lengthwise*

ONE Heat the canola and sesame oils in a nonstick sauté pan until hot. Add the shallot and garlic and stir-fry over medium heat for 1 minute until the shallot begins to turn transparent. **TWO** Turn up the heat to high. Add the chicken strips and stir-fry for about 5 minutes, or until cooked. **THREE** Quickly add the bean sprouts, bamboo shoots, crushed tomatoes, shoyu or tamari sauce, and scallions, and stir-fry for about 30 seconds until the bean sprouts have started to wilt slightly. **FOUR** Serve immediately.

Serves 4 with 2 other main dishes

NUTRIENT ANALYSIS PER SERVING 481 kJ – 114 cal – 15.5 g protein – 6.0 g carbohydrate – 3.7 g sugars – 3.4 g fat – 0.6 g saturated fat – 2.0 g fiber – 129 mg sodium

HEALTHY TIP Sprouted mung or other beans are great sources of vitamin C. A portion of bean sprouts will provide three-quarters of an adult's daily requirement. Sprouting increases the content of B vitamins in beans and also makes the protein easier to digest.

Sautéed chicken livers

Offal isn't to everyone's taste, but the addition of balsamic vinegar to this dish gives the sauce an added richness. Combined with melt-in-the-mouth chicken livers, even offalphobes will become great fans. Serve with Dry-fried Green Beans *(see page 126)* for a light meal.

INGREDIENTS *½ tablespoon canola or olive oil* ‖ *1 garlic clove, crushed* ‖ *1 slice fresh ginger root, peeled and roughly chopped* ‖ *2 shallots, sliced* ‖ *12 chicken livers, weighing about ½ pound, trimmed* ‖ *1 cup Chicken Stock (see page 17)* ‖ *1 teaspoon balsamic vinegar* ‖ *1 tablespoon rice wine or dry sherry* ‖ *2 teaspoons shoyu or tamari sauce*

ONE Heat the oil in a nonstick sauté pan or wok over a high heat until piping hot. Swirl the oil around the pan. Add the garlic, ginger, and shallots and stir-fry for a few seconds. **TWO** Add the chicken livers and cook for 1 minute on each side. **THREE** Add the stock, vinegar, rice wine, and shoyu sauce, and bring to a boil; then simmer for a couple of minutes until the stock has reduced and thickened.

Serves 4 with 2 other main dishes

NUTRIENT ANALYSIS PER SERVING 498 kJ – 119 cal – 17.4 g protein – 1.0 g carbohydrate – 0.5 g sugar – 5.0 g fat – 1.1 g saturated fat – 0.2 g fiber – 158 mg sodium

HEALTHY TIP Offal such as liver is an excellent source of iron and vitamin B12. However, it can be very high in cholesterol and vitamin A. Although vitamin A is needed for healthy skin and for immune function, concentrated sources such as liver should be avoided by women who are trying to conceive or who are already pregnant because high doses may lead to birth defects.

Kung Pao chicken

This is a popular dish in Szechwan, which is famous for its hot and spicy food. Apparently, it was a favorite of the governor in Szechwan during the Ching dynasty, in days of the last Emperor in the early 20th century, hence the name Kung Pao, meaning palace official. To make the most of the delicious spicy sauce, serve Sticky Rice *(see page 141)* with this dish.

INGREDIENTS *1 tablespoon canola or olive oil* ‖ *2–3 red chilies, deseeded and sliced* ‖ *2 garlic cloves, finely chopped* ‖ *¾ pound chicken breast, cut into ½-inch cubes* ‖ *1 teaspoon chili bean sauce* ‖ *2 ounces canned sliced bamboo shoots, drained* ‖ *2 ounces canned water chestnuts, drained* ‖ *1 tablespoon Chinese rice wine or dry sherry* ‖ *6½ tablespoons Chicken Stock (see page 17) or water* ‖ *½ cup roasted unsalted peanuts* ‖ *2 scallions, cut into ½-inch lengths*

CORNSTARCH PASTE *1 teaspoon cornstarch mixed with 1 tablespoon water*

ONE Heat the oil in a nonstick sauté pan over high heat. Add the chilies and garlic, and stir-fry for a few seconds. **TWO** Add the chicken and chili bean sauce and stir-fry for a couple of minutes; then add the bamboo shoots, water chestnuts, rice wine, and stock, and bring to a boil. Slowly add the cornstarch paste, stirring until the sauce has thickened and turned transparent. **THREE** Mix in the peanuts and scallions just before serving.

Serves 4 with 2 other main dishes

NUTRIENT ANALYSIS PER SERVING 941 kJ – 224 cal – 27.8 g protein – 5.8 g carbohydrate – 2.0 g sugars – 9.7 g fat – 1.6 g saturated fat – 1.1 g fiber – 85 mg sodium

HEALTHY TIP Nuts such as peanuts can be high in fat and calories, but a large proportion of their fat is in the healthy form of monounsaturated and polyunsaturated fats. Peanuts also are rich in essential fatty acids—omega-6 fats, which are important for normal growth and the development of body tissues.

Chicken and cashew nuts with vegetables

This dish is a firm favorite on the Chinese takeout menu. This low-fat version needs no oil as the chicken breast meat is simmered in stock, making it juicy and succulent. This dish goes well with Vegetarian Fried Rice *(see page 138)*.

INGREDIENTS *1 cup Chicken Stock (see page 17)* ‖ *¾ pound chicken breast, cubed* ‖ *2 tablespoons yellow bean sauce* ‖ *7 ounces carrots, sliced* ‖ *7 ounces bamboo shoots, sliced* ‖ *1¾ cups cashew nuts, toasted* ‖ *1 scallion, shredded*

CORNSTARCH PASTE *1 teaspoon cornstarch mixed with 2 tablespoons water or stock*

ONE Heat the chicken stock in a saucepan. Add the chicken meat and bring the liquid back to a boil, stirring. Lower the heat and cook for 5 minutes. Remove the chicken with a slotted spoon and set aside. **TWO** Add the yellow bean sauce and cook for a couple of minutes. Add the carrots and bamboo shoots, and cook for another couple of minutes. **THREE** Return the chicken to the pan, bring the sauce back to a boil, and thicken with cornstarch paste. **FOUR** Stir in the cashew nuts and scallion just before serving.

Serves 4 with 2 other main dishes.

NUTRIENT ANALYSIS PER SERVING 1549 kJ – 371 cal – 33.3 g protein – 15.2 g carbohydrate – 7.6 g sugars – 20.0 g fat – 4.1 g saturated fat – 3.3 g fiber – 268 mg sodium

HEALTHY TIP Cashew nuts are an excellent source of vitamin E and the B vitamins. Although their high fat content makes them calorific, the type of fat cashew nuts contain is mainly in the healthy form of unsaturated fatty acids.

Stir-fried chicken with lychees and melon

This is an adaptation of the winning recipe created by Mrs Jacky Williams in the Chinese Healthy Cooking Competition, which was jointly sponsored by the British Heart Foundation and the Chinese National Healthy Living Centre in London. Serve this dish with Sticky Rice *(see page 141)* and Stir-fried Tofu with Assorted Vegetables *(see page 115)*.

INGREDIENTS *½ teaspoon sesame oil ‖ 2 teaspoons cornstarch ‖ 2 teaspoons shoyu or tamari sauce ‖ ¾ pound chicken breast, cut into strips ‖ 1 medium honeydew melon ‖ 1 tablespoon canola or olive oil ‖ 1 garlic clove, crushed ‖ 2 slices fresh ginger root ‖ 3½ tablespoons Chicken Stock (see page 17) ‖ tablespoon honey ‖ 12–15 fresh lychees, peeled and pitted ‖ 2 scallions, sliced*

ONE Mix the sesame oil, cornstarch, and shoyu sauce, and rub into the chicken. Set aside for 10 minutes. **TWO** Cut the top off the melon and remove the seeds with a spoon. Scoop out the flesh with a teaspoon or a melon baller and set aside. You should now be left with a melon bowl. **THREE** Heat the oil in a nonstick sauté pan over a high heat. Add the garlic and ginger, and stir-fry for about 1 minute. **FOUR** Add the marinated chicken and stir-fry for about 3–4 minutes until lightly browned. Pour in the chicken stock and bring to a boil. **FIVE** Drizzle the honey over the chicken, then stir in the lychees and melon balls to warm them through. **SIX** Sprinkle with the scallions, then transfer the dish to the melon bowl to serve.

Serves 4

NUTRIENT ANALYSIS PER SERVING 915 kJ – 216 cal – 25.5 g protein – 19.9 g carbohydrate – 17.1 g sugar – 4.5 g fat – 0.8 g saturated fat – 1.1 g fiber – 186 mg sodium

HEALTHY TIP Melons are a good source of vitamin C. They also have a high water content which makes them efficient thirst-quenchers. Orange- and pink-fleshed varieties, such as cantaloupe melons, are also rich in beta carotene.

Lemon chicken

In this classic Cantonese dish the chicken is often deep-fried and served with a fairly thick lemon sauce. The chicken in this recipe is pan-fried and contains almost no sauce, only subtle overtones of fresh lemon juice and the lemon oil, which is released from the lemon rind as it cooks. Serve it with Shredded Beef with Carrots and Chili *(see page 45)* and stir-fried vegetables to celebrate a marriage of Cantonese and Szechwan cuisine.

INGREDIENTS *1 egg, lightly beaten* ‖ *2 garlic cloves, sliced* ‖ *2 small pieces of unwaxed lemon rind* ‖ *1 pound skinless chicken breast, cut into ¼-inch slices* ‖ *2 tablespoons cornstarch* ‖ *1 tablespoon canola or olive oil* ‖ *juice of 1 lemon* ‖ *1 scallion, chopped diagonally into ¾-inch lengths* ‖ *lemon slices, to garnish*

ONE Combine the egg, garlic, and lemon rind, and marinate the chicken for 10–15 minutes. **TWO** Remove the lemon rind and add the cornstarch to the marinated chicken. Mix thoroughly to distribute the cornstarch evenly among the chicken slices. **THREE** Heat the oil in a nonstick sauté pan over a high heat. Add the chicken slices, making sure you leave a little space between them. **FOUR** Fry the chicken slices for 2 minutes on each side. **FIVE** Reduce the heat to medium and stir-fry for 1 more minute, or until the chicken is browned and cooked. Turn up the heat and pour in the lemon juice. Add the scallion, garnish with lemon slices, and serve immediately.

Serves 4 with 2 other main dishes

NUTRIENT ANALYSIS PER SERVING 987 kJ – 234 cal – 32 g protein – 14.0 g carbohydrate – 0.1 g sugar – 5.8 g fat – 1.2 g saturated fat – 0.1 g fiber – 103 mg sodium

HEALTHY TIP Lemon juice is a great alternative seasoning to salt or soy sauce. Lemons are an excellent source of vitamin C, which can help to fight infection by maintaining a healthy immune system.

Sesame chicken with cucumber

This Szechwan dish is sometimes known as pang-pang or bon-bon chicken and usually contains a fiery mix of chili oil and chili flakes. The heat in this recipe comes from a subtle addition of mustard, which gives the chicken a slight tang without being too overpowering. Serve with a hearty bowl of Hot and Sour Soup *(see page 35)* and Steamed Buns *(see page 137)*.

INGREDIENTS *¾ pound cooked chicken breast, shredded* ‖ *¾ pound cucumber, sliced*

DRESSING *4 scallions, sliced* ‖ *4 teaspoons sesame paste* ‖ *1 tablespoon white wine vinegar* ‖ *2 teaspoons English mustard*

ONE Mix all the ingredients for the dressing in a large bowl. Add the shredded chicken and toss to mix thoroughly. **TWO** To serve, put the cucumber slices on a large serving plate and top with the dressed chicken.

Serves 4 as a light meal

NUTRIENT ANALYSIS PER SERVING 1117 kJ – 268 cal – 33.5 g protein – 2.2 g carbohydrate – 2.0 g sugars – 13.8 g fat – 2.8 g saturated fat – 1.9 g fiber – 195 mg sodium

HEALTHY TIP Cucumber has a high water content and is very low in calories, which makes it a great friend for anyone who is on a diet. Some people find raw cucumbers hard to digest, but in many Chinese recipes they are steamed or stir-fried, which softens the skin.

White-cut chicken

Use a good quality chicken for this classic Cantonese recipe, as it relies mostly on the texture and flavor of the chicken and is only slightly enhanced by the scallion and ginger dipping sauce. The chicken is gently poached so that the flesh remains succulent and flavorful. This dish goes well with Boiled Rice *(see page 140)* and Stir-fried Bok Choy with Shiitake Mushrooms *(see page 108)*. As alternative dipping sauces, the Pineapple Dipping Sauce *(see page 21)* and Chili Dipping Sauce *(see page 21)* would both go well.

INGREDIENTS *1 x 2-pound free-range chicken, cleaned and giblets removed*

DIPPING SAUCE *3 scallions, finely chopped ‖ 3 slices fresh ginger root, peeled and finely chopped ‖ 4 tablespoons chopped fresh cilantro ‖ 4 tablespoons shoyu or tamari sauce ‖ 1 teaspoon sesame oil ‖ 1 tablespoon lime juice ‖ 2 red chilies, deseeded and sliced*

ONE Put the chicken into a large pan of boiling water and bring it back to a boil. Cover the pan, turn down the heat to its lowest setting, and simmer for 20 minutes. Turn off the heat and leave the chicken to poach for another 20–25 minutes. **TWO** Remove the chicken from the pan and pour off the excess liquid. Leave to cool. **THREE** Combine all the ingredients for the dipping sauce in a small serving bowl. **FOUR** Cut the chicken into bite-sized pieces and serve with the dipping sauce.

Serves 4–6 with 2 other main dishes

NUTRIENT ANALYSIS PER SERVING WITH SAUCE 873 kJ – 208 cal – 32.6 g protein – 1.2 g carbohydrate – 0.3 g sugar – 8.1 g fat – 2.3 g saturated fat – 0.2 g fiber – 463 mg sodium

HEALTHY TIP Chicken is an excellent source of protein, which is essential for the repair of body tissues. It also contains a good supply of the B group vitamins that are needed for helping release energy from foods as well as for the healthy functioning of the nervous system. Chicken skin, however, is high in fat, so the weight-conscious should remove it before eating.

Fish and seafood

Sesame salmon with shredded vegetables

This simple recipe has a sesame theme, from the toasted sesame seeds adorning the top of the salmon to the Chinese sesame salt—gomasio—used for seasoning. Serve with Sticky Rice *(see page 141)* and Roasted Tofu with Szechwan Relish *(see page 106)* as an East meets West combination.

INGREDIENTS *1 pound thick salmon fillets, skinned* ‖ *1 tablespoon gomasio salt* ‖ *juice of ½ lime* ‖ *1 tablespoon raw sesame seeds* ‖ *1 large leek, shredded* ‖ *2 large carrots, shredded* ‖ *¼ pound snow peas, shredded*

ONE Put the salmon fillets in a foil-lined roasting pan and sprinkle with gomasi salt, lime juice, and sesame seeds. Cook in a preheated oven, 425°F, for 15–20 minutes, or until the salmon is just cooked and the sesame seeds are toasted and browned. **TWO** Meanwhile, toss together the leek, carrots, and snow peas and arrange on a serving dish. **THREE** To serve, place the salmon on the bed of vegetables and pour over the juices from the roasting pan.

Serves 4 with 2 other main dishes

NUTRIENT ANALYSIS PER SERVING 1126 kJ – 270 cal – 24.8 g protein – 7.7 g carbohydrate – 6.8 g sugars – 15.8 g fat – 2.7 g saturated fat – 3.0 g fiber – 111 mg sodium

HEALTHY TIP Oily fish, such as salmon and mackerel, contain omega-3 fatty acids, which are believed by health professionals to help protect against heart and circulation problems by improving the blood flow through blood vessels.

Spicy fish balls with sweet and sour sauce

Fish balls are found in most oriental supermarkets. They are generally made from a variety of shellfish and most are deep-fried, then vacuum-packed. In this recipe, they are simmered gently. Serve this dish at an impromptu finger food party with Sesame Shrimp Toasts *(see page 30)* and Fresh Spring Rolls *(see page 26)*.

INGREDIENTS *1 garlic clove, crushed* ‖ *2 teaspoons whole black peppercorns* ‖ *2 fresh red chilies, deseeded and sliced* ‖ *1 tablespoon fresh chives* ‖ *1 tablespoon fresh cilantro leaves* ‖ *1¼ pounds cod or haddock fillets, skinned and cut into large chunks* ‖ *1 egg white* ‖ *1 tablespoon cornstarch* ‖ *1 tablespoon shoyu or tamari sauce* ‖ *1 teaspoon sesame oil* ‖ *1 tablespoon chopped fresh cilantro, to garnish*

SWEET AND SOUR SAUCE *¾ cup Vegetable Stock (see page 17)* ‖ *5 tablespoons tomato ketchup* ‖ *1 tablespoon soft brown sugar* ‖ *1 slice fresh ginger root, peeled and finely chopped* ‖ *½ teaspoon hot pepper sauce*

CORNSTARCH PASTE *2 teaspoons cornstarch mixed with 3 tablespoons rice wine vinegar*

ONE Whizz the garlic, peppercorns, chilies, chives, and cilantro in a food processor. Add the fish fillets and egg white, and blend to a smooth paste. Add the cornstarch, shoyu sauce, and sesame oil, and blend for 1 minute. **TWO** Put a large saucepan of water on to boil. **THREE** Shape the fish mixture into balls about 1½ inches in diameter. **FOUR** Drop the fish balls into the boiling water, a few at a time; then bring the water back to a boil and simmer for about 5 minutes. Remove the fish balls with a slotted spoon and set aside. **FIVE** To make the sweet and sour sauce, put the stock, ketchup, sugar, ginger, and hot pepper sauce in a small saucepan. Bring to a boil, then stir in the cornstarch paste to thicken. Turn down the heat and simmer for 1 minute. **SIX** Put the fish balls on a shallow serving dish and sprinkle with the chopped cilantro. Pour the sauce into a small bowl and serve on the side.

Serves 4

NUTRIENT ANALYSIS PER SERVING 808 kJ – 191 cal – 30.1 g protein – 14.1 g carbohydrate – 4.3 g sugars – 2.1 g fat – 0.3 g saturated fat – 0.2 g fiber – 212 mg sodium

HEALTHY TIP You can use a mixture of white and oily fish for this recipe. If you don't like oily fish but still want to reap its nutritional benefits, this is a great way of introducing more omega-3 fats into your diet.

Sweet and sour shrimp

There are many regional variations of sweet and sour sauce; this Cantonese version uses a subtle blend of vinegar, sugar, and ketchup. The sauce is enhanced by adding lots of pineapple and green bell pepper, which gives an extra crunch to the dish.

INGREDIENTS *1 teaspoon olive oil* ∥ *1 garlic clove, chopped* ∥ *1 teaspoon chopped fresh ginger root* ∥ *⅔ cup Vegetable Stock (see page 17)* ∥ *1¼ cups chopped plum tomatoes* ∥ *1 tablespoon tomato ketchup* ∥ *1 tablespoon white wine vinegar* ∥ *1 tablespoon light muscavado (unrefined) sugar* ∥ *1 pound fresh or frozen raw shrimp, peeled and deveined* ∥ *5 ounces canned pineapple chunks, drained* ∥ *1¼ cups chopped green bell pepper* ∥ *1 scallion, chopped lengthwise*

CORNSTARCH PASTE *1 teaspoon cornstarch mixed with 6 tablespoons water or stock*

ONE Heat the oil in a nonstick pan. Add the garlic and ginger, and fry for about 20 seconds. **TWO** Add the stock, tomatoes, tomato ketchup, vinegar, and sugar, and bring to a boil. **THREE** Add the shrimp and cook for about 1 minute; then add the pineapple chunks and green bell pepper. Bring the mixture back to a boil and thicken with the cornstarch paste. **FOUR** Sprinkle with the scallion and serve immediately with Boiled Rice *(see page 140)*, or thin egg noodles to soak up the lovely sweet and sour sauce.

Serves 4 with 2 other main dishes

NUTRIENT ANALYSIS PER SERVING 742 kJ – 175 cal – 24.6 g protein – 15.4 g carbohydrate – 11.6 g sugars – 2.1 g fat – 0.4 g saturated fat – 1.3 g fiber – 1104 mg sodium

HEALTHY TIP Shellfish are generally high in protein, vitamins, and minerals, and have the added bonus of being low in calories. Shrimp are rich in the mineral selenium, which acts as an antioxidant by mopping up harmful free radicals in the body. There is scientific evidence to suggest that selenium protects against heart disease and some cancers.

Pan-seared king shrimp with ginger and scallions

Scallions and ginger are classic accompaniments to fish and shellfish dishes in Cantonese cuisine. This recipe uses both ingredients to create a quick and easy weekday lunch dish. This dish goes really well with Sweet and Sour Pork *(see page 53)*.

INGREDIENTS *½ tablespoon canola oil ‖ 2 garlic cloves, crushed ‖ 3–4 slices fresh ginger root, peeled and shredded ‖ ¾ pound large, raw shrimp (with shells), deveined ‖ 2 teaspoons shoyu or tamari sauce ‖ 2 teaspoons dry sherry ‖ ½ teaspoon sesame oil ‖ ½ teaspoon freshly ground black pepper ‖ 4 tablespoons Vegetable Stock (see page 17) ‖ 2 scallions, shredded into ¾-inch lengths, to serve*

CORNSTARCH PASTE *1 teaspoon cornstarch mixed with 1 tablespoon water*

ONE Heat the oil in a nonstick sauté pan and stir-fry the garlic and ginger for a few seconds. **TWO** Add the shrimp and stir-fry for about 1 minute until almost cooked. **THREE** Season with shoyu sauce, sherry, sesame oil, and pepper, and add the stock. Stir in the cornstarch paste to thicken the sauce. **FOUR** Sprinkle with the scallions and serve immediately.

Serves 4 with 2 other dishes

NUTRIENT ANALYSIS PER SERVING 423 kJ – 101 cal – 19.0 g protein – 0.9 g carbohydrate – 0.3 g sugars – 2.7 g fat – 0.4 g saturated fat – 0.2 g fiber – 274 mg sodium

HEALTHY TIP Ginger is a favorite spice in oriental cooking. In traditional Chinese medicine, it is thought to improve blood circulation and is also recommended as a cure for travel sickness and morning sickness.

Garlic steamed shrimp

This recipe for garlic lovers everywhere is ideal for cooking larger shrimp. Since you need to dig in with your fingers to enjoy this dish, you might as well go the whole hog and serve it with another dish that requires hands-on treatment, so try it with Mussels with Basil and Black Bean Sauce *(see page 94)* for the ultimate seafood experience.

INGREDIENTS *¾ pound large, raw shrimp (with shells), heads removed* ‖ *1 teaspoon olive oil* ‖ *4–5 garlic cloves, crushed* ‖ *1 teaspoon shoyu or tamari sauce* ‖ *1 teaspoon Chinese rice wine or dry sherry* ‖ *½ teaspoon ground black pepper* ‖ *1 tablespoon chopped fresh cilantro, to garnish*

ONE Using a pair of scissors, cut the shrimp down the back from the head to the tail end, to form a butterfly shape. Remove and discard the vein and arrange the shrimp in a circle on a heatproof dish. **TWO** Pour about 2 inches water into a wok, place a metal or wooden rack in the wok, and bring the water to a boil. **THREE** Mix the olive oil with the garlic, shoyu sauce, rice wine, and black pepper, and spoon over the shrimp. **FOUR** Put the heatproof dish on the rack, cover and steam over a high heat for 3 minutes, or until the shrimp have turned pink and are cooked. **FIVE** To serve, carefully remove the dish from the wok and scatter the cilantro leaves over the top.

Serves 4 with 2 other dishes

NUTRIENT ANALYSIS PER SERVING 363 kJ – 86 cal – 17.8 g protein – 0.4 g carbohydrate – 0.1 g sugars – 1.4 g fat – 0.2 g saturated fat – 0.1 g fiber – 191 mg sodium

HEALTHY TIP Some scientific studies have shown that daily doses of garlic may help to lower blood pressure and cholesterol. Garlic is also thought to have antiviral and antibacterial properties.

Oysters with black bean sauce

Oysters are often deep-fried in batter, which cooks them quickly, sealing in the natural juices. Although deep-fried oysters are delicious, they can also be high in fat. This low-fat version is pan-fried, which also ensures rapid cooking. In addition, their natural flavor is enhanced by garlic, scallions, and black bean sauce. Fish and shellfish meal combinations are common in Chinese restaurants. Try combining these oysters with Poached Scallops with Wasabi Dressing *(see page 96)* and Monkfish Stir-fried with Celery *(see page 100)*.

INGREDIENTS *1 tablespoon canola or olive oil ‖ 4 thin slices fresh ginger root ‖ 2 garlic cloves, crushed ‖ 2 tablespoons black bean sauce ‖ 24 oysters, shucked ‖ 4 scallions, diagonally sliced ‖ 1 tablespoon Chinese rice wine or dry sherry ‖ ½ teaspoon sesame oil*

ONE Heat the oil in a nonstick sauté pan or wok over a high heat. Add the ginger and garlic, and stir-fry for a few seconds until lightly browned. **TWO** Stir in the black bean sauce; then add the oysters. Cover the pan with a lid and cook the oysters over a high heat for 30 seconds. **THREE** Remove the lid and add the scallions, rice wine, and sesame oil. Stir and serve immediately.

Serves 4

NUTRIENT ANALYSIS PER SERVING 352 kJ – 84 cal – 7.4 g protein – 3.5 g carbohydrate – 1.3 g sugars – 4.1 g fat – 0.6 g saturated fat – 0.5 g fiber – 496 mg sodium

HEALTHY TIP Oysters have long been used as aphrodisiacs. Although the scientific basis for this is unclear, they are rich in the mineral zinc, which is needed for sperm production and a healthy libido.

Mixed seafood with bean thread noodles

Bean thread or cellophane noodles are lighter than rice vermicelli and have a firmer, more robust texture. They can absorb plenty of liquids and flavors. This dish goes well with Lemon-roasted Mackerel *(see page 99)* and some steamed rice.

INGREDIENTS *1 tablespoon canola or olive oil* ‖ *2 garlic cloves, chopped* ‖ *2 slices fresh ginger root, chopped* ‖ *1 tablespoon chili bean sauce* ‖ *2 teaspoons shoyu or tamari sauce* ‖ *1 teaspoon freshly ground white pepper* ‖ *4½ pints Fish Stock (see page 19) or Vegetable Stock (see page 17)* ‖ *½ pound Chinese leaves (po tsai), cut into 1-inch strips* ‖ *6 ounces dried bean thread or cellophane noodles* ‖ *¼ pound each raw shrimp, scallops, and squid* ‖ *1 tablespoon fresh cilantro leaves, to garnish*

ONE Heat the oil in a nonstick sauté pan or wok over a high heat until hot. Add the garlic and ginger, and stir-fry for a few seconds until fragrant. **TWO** Stir in the chili bean sauce, shoyu sauce, pepper, and stock, and bring to a boil. Add the Chinese leaves, turn down the heat to medium, and simmer for 10 minutes. **THREE** Add the bean thread noodles, cover the pan, and simmer for another 5 minutes. **FOUR** Add the mixed seafood, stir and bring back to a boil; then simmer for 1 more minute. Serve in a deep dish and garnish with cilantro leaves.

Serves 4–6 with 2 other dishes

NUTRIENT ANALYSIS PER SERVING 1116 kJ – 267 cal – 21.3 g protein – 36.7 g carbohydrate – 1.9 g sugars – 3.7 g fat – 0.5 g saturated fat – 0.8 g fiber – 315 mg sodium

HEALTHY TIP Bean thread noodles are made from mung beans and are often eaten as vegetables rather than as carbohydrate foods as rice or buckwheat noodles are.

Crab meat with asparagus

Crab can be overpowered by a sauce that is too rich or too spicy, but the light sauce in this recipe goes really well with it. The combination of crab and tender asparagus brings a mixture of sweetness and crunchiness to each mouthful. This dish goes well with Fu Yung with Vegetables *(see page 119)*.

INGREDIENTS *1 tablespoon canola or olive oil* ‖ *1 slice fresh ginger root* ‖ *1 garlic clove, crushed* ‖ *1 tablespoon Chinese rice wine or dry sherry* ‖ *6½ tablespoons Vegetable Stock (see page 17)* ‖ *1¼ pounds asparagus, trimmed, cut into pieces 1¼ inches long* ‖ *½ pound cooked crab meat* ‖ *1 teaspoon shoyu or tamari sauce* ‖ *2 scallions, thinly sliced, to serve*

CORNSTARCH PASTE *1 teaspoon cornstarch mixed with 5 tablespoons Vegetable Stock (see page 17) or water*

ONE Heat the oil in a nonstick sauté pan over a high heat. Add the ginger and garlic, and stir-fry for a few seconds. **TWO** Pour in the wine and stock and bring to a boil. Add the asparagus and cook over a high heat for 2–3 minutes; then remove with a slotted spoon to a serving plate. **THREE** Add the crab meat and shoyu sauce. Bring the mixture back to a boil, and slowly add the cornstarch paste, stirring continuously until the sauce has thickened. **FOUR** To serve, spoon the crab sauce over the asparagus and sprinkle with the scallions.

Serves 4 with 2 other main dishes

NUTRIENT ANALYSIS PER SERVING 642kJ – 154 cal – 16.8g protein – 5.8g carbohydrate – 3.0g sugars – 7.1g fat – 1.0g saturated fat – 2.7g fiber – 308mg sodium

HEALTHY TIP Asparagus is a rich source of the B vitamin folate. A 3½-ounce serving provides three-quarters of an adult's daily requirement of folate, which is needed for making healthy blood. It is also valuable for pregnant women to help reduce the risk of having babies with neural tube defects.

Tomato shrimp with mango

Fresh shrimp are particularly sought in Cantonese cooking. Tomato and shrimp are a classic combination; this recipe also includes a mango, which adds an exotic tropical flavor. This robustly flavored dish should be served with another shellfish dish with equally strong flavors, such as Oysters with Black Bean Sauce *(see page 85)*.

INGREDIENTS *1 tablespoon canola or olive oil* ‖ *2 garlic cloves, crushed* ‖ *2 slices fresh ginger root, peeled and finely chopped* ‖ *1 teaspoon chili oil* ‖ *2 tablespoons tomato ketchup* ‖ *¾ pound raw shrimp, peeled and deveined* ‖ *4 tomatoes, chopped* ‖ *1 large mango, skinned and cubed* ‖ *2 scallions, sliced*

ONE Heat the oil in a nonstick sauté pan over a high heat. Swirl the oil around the pan and add the garlic and ginger. Stir-fry for a couple of minutes over a medium to high heat until the garlic has browned slightly. **TWO** Add the chili oil and tomato ketchup, and stir-fry for 2–3 minutes. **THREE** Add the shrimp and stir-fry for 3–4 minutes, or until they have turned pink. Mix in the tomatoes and mango, and warm through. **FOUR** To serve, sprinkle with the scallions.

Serves 4 with 2 other main dishes

NUTRIENT ANALYSIS PER SERVING 627 kJ – 148 cal – 18.9 g protein – 10.6 g carbohydrate – 10.1 g sugars – 3.8 g fat – 0.6 g saturated fat – 2.0 g fiber – 328 mg sodium

HEALTHY TIP Mangoes are excellent sources of vitamin C, carotenoids, fiber, and potassium. Some studies show that they have the ability to improve general health and boost immunity.

Squid stir-fried with snow peas

Fresh squid has an intense sweet flavor, which is further enhanced by combining it with fresh, crispy snow peas in this dish. Seasonings are kept quite light, with the Szechwan peppercorns adding a subtle but clean citrus flavor. This dish goes well with stir-fried chicken dishes and stir-fried green beans.

INGREDIENTS *½ pound squid, cleaned* ‖ *1 tablespoon canola or olive oil* ‖ *1 green chili, chopped* ‖ *2 teaspoons Szechwan peppercorns, crushed* ‖ *2 garlic cloves, crushed* ‖ *1 small onion, chopped* ‖ *½ pound snow peas* ‖ *2 teaspoons shoyu or tamari sauce* ‖ *1 tablespoon Chinese rice wine or dry sherry*

ONE Cut the squid into slices and score with a criss-cross pattern (this makes them curl up when they are cooked, and the grooves help to trap the sauce). **TWO** Heat the oil in a nonstick sauté pan over a high heat until hot. Add the chili, peppercorns, garlic, and onion, and stir-fry over a medium heat for about 3–4 minutes. **THREE** Turn the heat to high, add the squid slices, and stir-fry quickly for 1 minute; then remove them from the pan. **FOUR** Toss in the snow peas and stir-fry for 1 minute; then return the squid to the pan. Stir to mix, add the shoyu and rice wine, and stir-fry for a few seconds; then serve immediately.

Serves 2 with another main dish

NUTRIENT ANALYSIS PER SERVING 450 kJ – 107 cal – 12.3 g protein – 4.8 g carbohydrate – 3.0 g sugars – 4.0 g fat – 0.6 g saturated fat – 1.7 g fiber – 154 mg sodium

HEALTHY TIP Squid is a good source of the mineral selenium. Selenium is needed for healthy hair and skin and there is some scientific evidence that it helps to protect against prostate cancer.

Pan-fried bream fillets with oriental dressing

Fresh bream is a favorite fish in the orient because of its firm texture and sweet taste. It can be steamed or baked whole, but this recipe uses fillets for convenience. Pan-frying makes the skin wonderfully crispy and aromatic, and the sweetness of the flesh is enhanced by the subtle flavor of the dressing. This dish goes well with Vegetarian Fried Rice *(see page 138)* and Dry-fried Green Beans *(see page 126)*.

INGREDIENTS *1 tablespoon canola or olive oil* ‖ *4 x 6-ounce red or black bream fillets* ‖ *4 garlic cloves, crushed* ‖ *juice of 1 lemon* ‖ *1 tablespoon chopped Thai basil leaves, to garnish*

DRESSING *1 tablespoon Lemon and Fish Sauce (see page 19)* ‖ *3 tablespoons Fish Stock (see page 19)*

ONE Heat the oil in a nonstick sauté pan over a high heat until piping hot. **TWO** Add the bream fillets skin-side down and fry for 2 minutes. Turn the fillets over and put the garlic between the pieces of fish. Fry for 1 more minute, then add the lemon juice and cook until it has almost evaporated. Transfer the fish fillets to a serving plate. **THREE** To make the dressing, mix the lemon and fish sauce with the fish stock. Drizzle the dressing over the fish fillets and garnish with the Thai basil leaves.

Serves 4 with 2 other main dishes

NUTRIENT ANALYSIS PER SERVING 836 kJ – 199 cal – 30.9 g protein – 1.3 g carbohydrate – 1.0 g sugars – 7.9g fat – 0.4 g saturated fat – 0 g fiber – 330 mg sodium

HEALTHY TIP Bream is a white fish that is low in fat and high in protein and vitamin B12. It is ideal for people who are watching their weight.

Steamed trout with black beans

Fermented black beans, if you can find them, are great for enhancing the taste of trout, but you can use 1 tablespoon black bean sauce instead. This dish goes well with Bamboo Shoots and Straw Mushrooms with Broccoli *(see page 123).*

INGREDIENTS *1 teaspoon fermented black beans* ‖ *2 slices fresh ginger root, peeled and finely chopped* ‖ *2 garlic cloves, finely chopped* ‖ *2 scallions, sliced* ‖ *1 teaspoon shoyu or tamari sauce* ‖ *1 teaspoon olive oil* ‖ *¾ pound trout fillets, cut into pieces* ‖ *1 tablespoon roughly chopped fresh cilantro, to garnish*

ONE Pour about 2 inches water into a wok, place a metal or wooden rack in the wok, and bring the water to a boil. **TWO** Meanwhile, rinse the black beans in water to get rid of the excess salt. Put them into a small bowl and mash lightly with a fork. Mix in the ginger, garlic, scallions, shoyu sauce, and olive oil. **THREE** Place the fish pieces in a heatproof serving dish and thoroughly stir in the black bean sauce mixture, to ensure that all the fish pieces are coated. **FOUR** Set the dish on the wok rack, cover the wok, and steam over a high heat for 6–8 minutes, or until the fish is cooked. Sprinkle with cilantro leaves and serve immediately.

Serves 4 with 2 other main dishes

NUTRIENT ANALYSIS PER SERVING 547 kJ – 130 cal – 18.2 g protein – 2.1 g carbohydrate – 1.2 g sugars – 5.5 g fat – 1.1 g saturated fat – 0.3 g fiber – 271 mg sodium

HEALTHY TIP Trout is an oily fish, which is an excellent source of omega-3 fatty acids. Some scientific studies have shown that oily fish may help to relieve some of the symptoms of psoriasis.

Mussels with basil and black bean sauce

An oriental version of *moules marinière*, this fragrant and spicy dish is great on a cold, wintry night. Serve as a light lunch with Rice Noodles with Aromatic Shrimp *(see page 134)*.

INGREDIENTS *1 tablespoon canola or olive oil* ‖ *½ teaspoon freshly ground black pepper* ‖ *2 red chilies, deseeded and sliced* ‖ *2 garlic cloves, crushed* ‖ *2 pounds mussels, scrubbed and debearded* ‖ *4 tablespoons Fish Stock (see page 19)* ‖ *1 tablespoon black bean sauce* ‖ *1 tablespoon Chinese rice wine or dry sherry* ‖ *large handful of fresh cilantro leaves* ‖ *large handful of fresh Thai basil leaves*

ONE Heat the oil in a wok over a high heat until hot. Add the pepper, chilies, and garlic, and stir-fry for about 30 seconds until fragrant. **TWO** Add the mussels and stir to mix; then add the stock, black bean sauce, and rice wine. Cover the pan and cook for about 2 minutes until the mussels have opened. **THREE** Toss in the cilantro and basil leaves, then transfer the mussels to a large serving dish, discarding any that have not opened. Serve immediately.

Serves 4–6 with 2 other main dishes

NUTRIENT ANALYSIS PER SERVING 927 kJ – 221 cal – 30.8 g protein – 7.2 g carbohydrate – 0.5 g sugars – 7.4 g fat – 1.4 g saturated fat – 0.1 g fiber – 821 mg sodium

HEALTHY TIP Mussels are a rich source of the minerals iodine and iron. Shellfish are the best source of iodine, which is needed to make thyroid hormones that control the rate at which the body uses energy.

Poached scallops with wasabi dressing

Fresh scallops are a particular favorite in Cantonese cooking. This recipe is ideal for king scallops; poaching them in stock ensures gentle cooking and preserves their sweet succulent flavor. Wasabi paste is a Japanese mustard, so pungent that it's been nicknamed "namida" or "tears" in traditional sushi bars. So, be warned. This dish goes well with Vegetable Chop Suey *(see page 122)* for a light and quick supper.

INGREDIENTS *2½ pints Fish Stock (see page 19)* ‖ *16 king scallops, shelled*

DRESSING *1 teaspoon wasabi paste* ‖ *3½ tablespoons fish stock from above* ‖ *2 teaspoons shoyu or tamari sauce* ‖ *½ tablespoon extra virgin olive oil*

ONE Heat the stock in a saucepan until boiling. Add the scallops and cover the pan; then turn off the heat and let the scallops poach for 2–3 minutes, depending how thick they are. Transfer the scallops to a serving dish with a slotted spoon. **TWO** To make the dressing, combine the wasabi paste, stock, shoyu sauce, and oil, and drizzle over the scallops.

Serves 4 with 2 other main dishes

NUTRIENT ANALYSIS PER SERVING 423 kJ – 100 cal – 16.5 g protein – 3.2 g carbohydrate – 0 g sugars – 2.5 g fat – 0.5 g saturated fat – 0 g fiber – 210 mg sodium

HEALTHY TIP Scallops are a good source of potassium, which is needed for maintaining fluid balance in the body, although too much is inadvisable for people with kidney problems.

Steamed sea bass with scallion and ginger dressing

Traditionally, Chinese people prefer whole fish to fillets. This recipe is simpler to eat and there's no need to worry about bones. Other fish that can be used as a variation include turbot and halibut. Chinese people often combine delicate fish dishes with other equally subtle flavors, so try this with White-cut Chicken *(see page 75)* and stir-fried vegetables for a low-fat meal.

INGREDIENTS *4 x 6-ounce sea bass fillets* ‖ *1 tablespoon canola oil* ‖ *4 scallions, finely shredded* ‖ *4 slices fresh ginger root, peeled and finely shredded* ‖ *2 tablespoons Fish Stock (see page 19)* ‖ *2 teaspoons shoyu or tamari sauce* ‖ *2 teaspoons Chinese rice wine or dry sherry*

ONE Half-fill a wok with water, place a metal or wooden rack in the wok, and bring the water to a boil over a high heat. **TWO** Meanwhile, put the sea bass fillets on a shallow plate and put it on the rack as soon as the water has boiled. Cover the wok and steam the sea bass over a high heat for 7–8 minutes. **THREE** To prepare the sauce, heat the oil in a small saucepan over a medium heat. Add the scallions and ginger, and stir-fry for a few seconds; then add the stock, shoyu sauce, and rice wine. Stir and cook for a few more seconds, then remove the pan from the heat. **FOUR** Remove the steamed fillets from the wok and pour the warm dressing over them. Serve immediately.

Serves 4 with 2 other main dishes

NUTRIENT ANALYSIS PER SERVING 874 kJ – 208 cal – 34.2 g protein – 0.9 g carbohydrate – 0.4 g sugars – 7.2 g fat – 0.9 g saturated fat – 0.2 g fiber – 205 mg sodium

HEALTHY TIP Steaming is a convenient and delicious way of cooking food without adding oil. Foods are cooked gently and evenly because the heat doesn't rise above boiling point.

Lemon-roasted mackerel

The mackerel belongs to the tuna family and, when fresh, its skin has a bluish-green metallic sheen. Choose large fillets for this recipe. Roasting releases rich aromatic oils from the fresh mackerel, which are complemented perfectly by sharpness of the lemon juice.

INGREDIENTS *2 garlic cloves, crushed ‖ 2 slices fresh ginger root, peeled and finely chopped ‖ ½ teaspoon freshly ground black pepper ‖ ½ tablespoon olive oil ‖ juice of 1 lemon ‖ 1 teaspoon shoyu or tamari sauce ‖ 2 x 7½-ounce mackerel fillets ‖ 2 scallions, finely chopped*

ONE Mix together the garlic, ginger, pepper, olive oil, the juice of half the lemon, and the shoyu sauce in a small bowl. **TWO** Put the mackerel fillets into a foil-lined roasting pan, skin-side down, and spoon the marinade over them. Put the pan in a preheated oven, 475°F, and cook for 15 minutes until the fillets are crisp and golden. **THREE** Put the fillets on a serving plate, sprinkle with the remaining lemon juice and the scallions, and serve immediately. Serve with plain rice noodles or rice to soak up the garlicky lemon sauce.

Serves 4 with 2 other main dishes

NUTRIENT ANALYSIS PER SERVING 1356 kJ – 321 cal – 26.1 g protein – 0.9 g carbohydrate – 0.4 g sugars – 23.7 g fat – 4.8 g saturated fat – 0.2 g fiber – 129 mg sodium

HEALTHY TIP Mackerel is an oily fish and an excellent source of omega-3 fats. Scientific research has shown that oily fish has an anti-inflammatory effect on the body. Some migraine sufferers have found that eating more fatty fish helps them on a long-term basis.

Monkfish stir-fried with celery

Monkfish has a firm texture and virtually no small bones, which makes it ideal for stir-frying or braising. The juices from the monkfish combine with the distinctive taste of celery to give this dish a unique flavor. Serve with Roast Pork *(see page 56)*, stir-fried vegetables, and a tofu dish for a family get-together.

INGREDIENTS *1 tablespoon canola or olive oil* ‖ *3 slices fresh ginger root* ‖ *1 pound monkfish fillets, cut into ½-inch thick slices* ‖ *6½ tablespoons hot Fish Stock (see page 19)* ‖ *1 teaspoon shoyu or tamari sauce* ‖ *1 tablespoon Chinese rice wine or dry sherry* ‖ *1 teaspoon freshly ground white pepper* ‖ *½ teaspoon sesame oil* ‖ *1 pound tender celery hearts, cut into 1-inch x ½-inch pieces*

CORNSTARCH PASTE *2 teaspoons cornstarch mixed with 2 tablespoons water or stock*

ONE Heat the oil in a nonstick sauté pan over a high heat. Add the ginger and stir-fry for a few seconds until fragrant. **TWO** Add the monkfish and stir-fry for 1 minute; then add the hot stock and bring to a boil. Add the shoyu sauce, rice wine, pepper, and sesame oil, and stir. **THREE** Add the celery and bring the mixture back to a boil; then add the cornstarch paste, stirring until the sauce has thickened and has turned translucent.

Serves 4 with 2 other main dishes

NUTRIENT ANALYSIS PER SERVING 552 kJ – 130 cal – 18.4 g protein – 5.0 g carbohydrate – 1.2 g sugars – 3.9 g fat – 0.6 g saturated fat – 1.3 g fiber – 132 mg sodium

HEALTHY TIP Celery contains phenolic acids, which have been shown to have anti-cancer effects; they have the ability to block the action of hormones called prostaglandins, which promote the growth of tumors.

Vegetarian

Red Thai curry with tofu and mixed vegetables

There are three types of Thai curry—red, green, and yellow—each made with different colored chilies. Traditional Thai curries are made with whole coconut milk, which is high in fat. This recipe uses a reduced-fat version, but the end result is still deliciously creamy. To continue the Southeast Asian theme, begin your meal with Fresh Spring Rolls *(see page 26)* or Shrimp and Grapefruit Salad *(see page 32)* as a starter.

INGREDIENTS *1 tablespoon canola or olive oil* ‖ *2 tablespoons red curry paste* ‖ *1–2 fresh green chilies, deseeded and sliced* ‖ *¾ cup plus 1 tablespoon canned light coconut milk* ‖ *1 cup Vegetable Stock (see page 17)* ‖ *1 large eggplant, diced* ‖ *12 baby corn* ‖ *3½ ounces snow peas* ‖ *3½ ounces carrots, sliced* ‖ *¼ pound fresh shiitake mushrooms, halved* ‖ *1 large green bell pepper, cored, deseeded, and sliced* ‖ *5 ounces canned sliced bamboo shoots, drained* ‖ *1 tablespoon Thai fish sauce* ‖ *1 tablespoon clear honey* ‖ *2 kaffir lime leaves* ‖ *1 x 14-ounce package silken firm tofu, cut into 2-inch cubes*

TO SERVE *large handful of torn Thai basil leaves* ‖ *handful of toasted cashew nuts*

ONE Heat the oil in a large saucepan and fry the red curry paste and chilies for 1 minute; then stir in 2 tablespoons coconut milk (from the thicker part, which is at the top of the can) and cook, stirring constantly, for 2 minutes. **TWO** Add the vegetable stock and bring to a boil. Toss in the eggplant, then bring the mixture back to a boil and simmer for about 5 minutes. Add the remaining vegetables and cook for another 5–10 minutes. Stir in the fish sauce, honey, lime leaves, and the remaining coconut milk, and simmer for another 5 minutes, stirring occasionally. Add the tofu cubes and mix well. **THREE** To serve, top with the torn Thai basil leaves and toasted cashew nuts. Jasmine or Sticky Rice *(see page 141)* goes best with this curry to absorb all the wonderful aromatic sauce.

Serves 4 with 2 other main dishes

NUTRIENT ANALYSIS PER SERVING 862 kJ – 254 cal – 13.3 g protein – 13.8 g carbohydrate – 11.0 g sugars – 16.3 g fat – 5.7 g saturated fat – 4.8 g fiber – 482 mg sodium

HEALTHY TIP Mushrooms are a good source of potassium, which is needed for maintaining fluid balance in the body. They are low in calories but not if they are fried in oil. In traditional Chinese medicine, shiitake mushrooms are believed to bring a long and healthy life.

Roasted tofu with Szechwan relish

Children sometimes dislike the blandness of tofu, but they will often eat it if it's served with a really flavorsome and colorful sauce. This recipe takes its inspiration from Mexico; the relish is reminiscent of salsa and the crispy tofu cubes are not unlike tortilla chips. For a meal with a spicy theme, serve Hot and Sour Soup *(see page 35)* as a starter before this dish.

INGREDIENTS *1½ tablespoons olive oil* ‖ *1 x 14-ounce package of silken firm tofu, cut into 1-inch cubes*

SZECHWAN RELISH *½ pound fresh tomatoes, diced* ‖ *1 cup diced cucumber* ‖ *1 red chili, deseeded and sliced* ‖ *2 tablespoons thinly sliced scallions* ‖ *½ garlic clove, crushed* ‖ *½ teaspoon soft brown sugar* ‖ *1 tablespoon lime juice* ‖ *2 tablespoons chopped fresh cilantro* ‖ *½ teaspoon freshly ground black pepper*

ONE Pour the olive oil into a large foil-lined roasting pan and spread it with a brush. Arrange the tofu cubes evenly over the oil. **TWO** Put the roasting pan on the top shelf of a preheated oven, 475°F, and roast for about 15–20 minutes, or until the tofu is crisp and golden brown. **THREE** Meanwhile, make the Szechwan relish. Combine all the ingredients in a bowl and mix well. Set aside. **FOUR** Put the roasted tofu cubes on a serving dish and spoon over the relish.

Serves 4

NUTRIENT ANALYSIS PER SERVING 536 kJ – 129 cal – 9.0 g protein – 3.9 g carbohydrate – 3.4 g sugars – 8.7 g fat – 1.2 g saturated fat – 0.9 g fiber – 12 mg sodium

HEALTHY TIP You can further reduce the amount of oil you cook with by limiting yourself to a squirt from a reduced-calorie spray and pan-frying the tofu cubes in a nonstick sauté pan. This will make a great low-fat snack.

Stir-fried cabbage

Conical or sweetheart cabbages are seldom used in the oriental kitchen. Spring greens are the only member of the cabbage family to be used much, because they are shredded and deep-fried to make crispy seaweed. This recipe is very simple but tasty and delicious. The crunchy texture of this stir-fried cabbage goes very well with roasted or broiled meat dishes such as Chandoori Chicken *(see page 62)* and Pork Satay *(see page 57)*.

INGREDIENTS *½ tablespoon canola oil* ‖ *2 garlic cloves, crushed* ‖ *1 pound conical cabbage, finely shredded* ‖ *6½ tablespoons Vegetable Stock (see page 17)* ‖ *2 teaspoons shoyu or tamari sauce* ‖ *½ teaspoon freshly ground black pepper*

ONE Heat the oil in a nonstick sauté pan over a high heat until piping hot. **TWO** Add the garlic and stir-fry for a few seconds until browned. Add the cabbage and stir; then add the stock and shoyu sauce. Cover the pan and cook for a couple of minutes. **THREE** Remove the lid and continue cooking until all the stock has evaporated, stirring from time to time. **FOUR** Stir in the black pepper and serve immediately.

Serves 4 with 2 other main dishes

NUTRIENT ANALYSIS PER SERVING 203 kJ – 49 cal – 2.4 g protein – 5.6 g carbohydrate – 5.0 g sugars – 2.0 g fat – 0.3 g saturated fat – 3.1 g fiber – 90 mg sodium

HEALTHY TIP Eaten raw or lightly cooked, cabbage is an excellent source of vitamin C. Many scientific studies have found that cabbage contains plant chemicals that may be protective against certain cancers, such as colon, breast, and ovarian cancer.

Stir-fried bok choy with shiitake mushrooms

This dish goes very well with many of the main-course recipes. For a variation, instead of bok choy, you can use broccoli or another Chinese vegetable such as choy sum (Chinese flowering cabbage) or kai lan (Chinese mustard greens). This dish goes very well with Steamed Trout with Black Beans *(see page 93)*.

INGREDIENTS *½ tablespoon canola or olive oil* ‖ *1 pound bok choy, halved lengthwise* ‖ *20 fresh shiitake mushrooms, halved* ‖ *1 teaspoon shoyu or tamari sauce* ‖ *1 tablespoon Chinese rice wine or dry sherry* ‖ *3 tablespoons Vegetable Stock (see page 17)*

CORNSTARCH PASTE *½ tablespoon cornstarch mixed with 1 tablespoon water*

ONE Heat the canola oil in a nonstick sauté pan over a high heat until it is piping hot, swirling it round to cover the base of the pan. **TWO** Add the bok choy, a handful at a time, stirring occasionally. Cover the pan and cook for about 2–3 minutes, until the bok choy leaves have wilted slightly. Remove to a serving plate. **THREE** Return the pan to the heat and add the shiitake mushrooms. Stir-fry over a high heat for 30 seconds. Add the shoyu sauce, rice wine, and vegetable stock, and stir to mix. Add the cornstarch paste slowly, stirring constantly until the sauce has thickened. **FOUR** Pour the mushrooms and sauce over the bok choy and serve immediately.

Serves 4 with 2 other main dishes

NUTRIENT ANALYSIS PER SERVING 343 kJ – 83 cal – 7.3 g protein – 7.3 g carbohydrate – 3.4 g sugar – 2.3 g fat – 0.3 g saturated fat – 4.8 g fiber – 439 mg sodium

HEALTHY TIP Some vegetables can be eaten raw in salads, but bok choy isn't one of them; cooking makes it taste much sweeter and juicier. Stir-frying vegetables for a short time ensures that they retain most of their vitamins and minerals; boiling them destroys over half of their vitamin C content.

Chili kale

Kale is often maligned for being woody and inedible. Take time to pick over the kale leaves and chose young leaves wherever you can. Don't forget to remove the woody stalks when you're preparing them for this dish. This dish is best served with a hearty casserole such as Spiced Beef and Vegetable Stew *(see page 50)*.

INGREDIENTS *1 tablespoon olive oil* ‖ *1 garlic clove, crushed* ‖ *1 large white onion, chopped* ‖ *1 pound curly kale, stalks removed and leaves chopped* ‖ *2 teaspoons lime juice* ‖ *1 red chili, deseeded and chopped* ‖ *1 teaspoon gomasio salt* ‖ *½ teaspoon freshly ground black pepper*

ONE Heat the oil in a pan. Add the garlic and onion, and sauté for about 10 minutes, or until the onion is translucent. **TWO** Add the curly kale and stir-fry for about 5 minutes. **THREE** Stir in the lime juice and red chili. Season with gomasio salt and pepper to taste, and serve immediately.

Serves 4 with 2 other main dishes

NUTRIENT ANALYSIS PER SERVING 414 kJ – 98 cal – 9.1 g protein – 6.8 g carbohydrate – 5.4 g sugars – 4.1 g fat – 0.5 g saturated fat – 8.3 g fiber – 150 mg sodium

HEALTHY TIP Kale is a good source of calcium, which is needed for strong bones and teeth, as well as for the healthy functioning of our nerves and muscles.

Sesame broccoli

Very young children often refer to broccoli as "trees" and even though it is a vegetable, many enjoy it if it is quickly blanched. There is a more of an adult theme in this recipe in which blanched broccoli is dressed with a wonderful sauce made of sesame seeds, sesame oil, garlic, and shoyu or tamari sauce. For a complete vegetarian meal, try this dish with Lentils with Lemon Grass and Lime Leaves *(see page 116)* and steamed or Boiled Rice *(see page 140)*.

INGREDIENTS *1 pound broccoli florets* ‖ *1 teaspoon sesame oil* ‖ *1 tablespoon shoyu or tamari sauce* ‖ *1 garlic clove, crushed* ‖ *1 tablespoon toasted sesame seeds*

ONE Blanch the broccoli florets in a saucepan of boiling water for a couple of minutes; then drain and place on a serving dish. **TWO** Make a dressing with the sesame oil, shoyu sauce, and crushed garlic, and pour it over broccoli. **THREE** Just before serving, sprinkle with the sesame seeds.

Serves 4 with 2 other main dishes

NUTRIENT ANALYSIS PER SERVING 286 kJ – 69 cal – 6.3 g protein – 2.7 g carbohydrate – 1.9 g sugars – 3.6 g fat – 0.6 g saturated fat – 3.6 g fiber – 136 mg sodium

HEALTHY TIP Broccoli is an excellent source of vitamin C and beta carotene. It also contains useful amounts of folate, iron, and potassium. Like all other vegetables, these essential water-soluble vitamins are easily destroyed by heat or in their cooking water. Preserve vitamins and minerals by cooking vegetables for the shortest possible time and use a minimal amount of water if you're going to boil them.

Stir-fried spicy tempeh with vegetables

This dish takes its inspiration from Indonesia where tempeh (fermented soy beans) is often used as a protein alternative to meat, fish, and eggs. Serve this dish with boiled whole-wheat or egg noodles and eat it like a thick laksa.

INGREDIENTS *1 tablespoon canola or olive oil* ‖ *2 fresh red chilies, sliced* ‖ *2 lemon grass stalks, finely sliced* ‖ *2 kaffir lime leaves* ‖ *1 large garlic clove, crushed* ‖ *2 slices fresh ginger root, peeled and chopped* ‖ *1 tablespoon tamarind paste* ‖ *2 tablespoons Vegetable Stock (see page 17)* ‖ *2 teaspoons shoyu or tamari sauce* ‖ *1 tablespoon clear honey* ‖ *1 pound tempeh, cut into strips* ‖ *¼ pound baby corn* ‖ *¼ pound asparagus, halved*

ONE Heat the oil in a nonstick sauté pan or wok over a high heat until piping hot. Swirl it around the pan; then add the chilies, lemon grass, lime leaves, garlic, and ginger. Turn the heat down to medium and stir-fry the spices for about 2–3 minutes. **TWO** Add the tamarind, vegetable stock, shoyu sauce, and honey, and cook for about 2–3 minutes until the sauce is thick and glossy. **THREE** Add the tempeh, corn, and asparagus, and stir-fry for about 2 minutes to warm them through.

Serves 4 with 2 other main dishes

NUTRIENT ANALYSIS PER SERVING 1185 kJ – 282 cal – 27.0 g protein – 18.1 g carbohydrate – 10.6 g sugars – 11.1 g fat – 0.4 g saturated fat – 6.6 g fiber – 111 mg sodium

HEALTHY TIP Tamarind trees produce sickle-shaped pods with a fruity pulp, which has a slightly sharp and sour flavor. Tamarind paste is a concentrated form of pulp that can be used to flavor soups, salads, curries, meat, and fish dishes. It is rich in vitamin C and fiber. In folk medicine, tamarind is thought to act as a laxative and as an antiseptic.

Ma-po tofu

This dish comes from Szechwan. It is traditionally cooked with ground beef or pork; this is a vegetarian version, but it still has the robust flavors of the original. The tofu acts like a sponge, soaking up the spices, so this dish tastes even better the day after you've made it. The spicy sauce in this dish is best appreciated with plain rice.

INGREDIENTS *5–6 dried Chinese mushrooms* ‖ *1 tablespoon canola or olive oil* ‖ *2 garlic cloves, crushed* ‖ *2 fresh red chilies, deseeded and sliced* ‖ *1¼ cups Vegetable Stock (see page 17)* ‖ *½ tablespoon hoisin sauce* ‖ *½ tablespoon yellow bean sauce* ‖ *1 tablespoon shoyu or tamari sauce* ‖ *1 x 14-ounce package silken firm tofu, cubed* ‖ *3 scallions, thinly sliced, to garnish*

CORNSTARCH PASTE *2 teaspoons cornstarch mixed with 2 tablespoons water*

ONE Put the dried mushrooms in a heatproof bowl. Cover with boiling water and put a plate over the top of the bowl to keep the steam in. Set aside for 20–30 minutes. Drain the mushrooms and remove the stalks; then squeeze the water out of the caps and chop them roughly. **TWO** Heat the oil in a nonstick pan or wok until piping hot. Add the garlic and chilies, and stir-fry for a few seconds over a medium high heat. **THREE** Add the stock, hoisin, and yellow bean and shoyu sauces. Stir well and simmer for another few minutes. **FOUR** Gently mix in the tofu and cook for a few minutes to heat through. **FIVE** Add the cornstarch paste to the sauce, stirring gently to thicken. **SIX** To serve, sprinkle with the scallions.

Serves 4 with 2 other main dishes

NUTRIENT ANALYSIS PER SERVING 548 kJ – 132 cal – 9.1 g protein – 7.9 g carbohydrate – 0.6 g sugars – 7.2 g fat – 0.9 g saturated fat – 0.2 g fiber – 197 mg sodium

HEALTHY TIP Tofu is made by grinding cooked soy beans with water. It is then strained and mixed with gypsum (calcium sulphate) to solidify it into a curd. It is, therefore, an excellent source of calcium, particularly for people from the Far East who drink little milk and don't eat dairy products regularly.

Stir-fried tofu with assorted vegetables

This is another classic way of serving tofu. The tofu is often deep-fried first to give it extra crispness; this adds more fat and calories, but it does taste delicious. You can achieve a similar crunchiness by roasting the tofu cubes with a little olive oil, then stir-frying them with the rest of the ingredients. Serve this dish with steamed rice and Sea-spiced Eggplants *(see page 124)*.

INGREDIENTS *1 tablespoon olive or canola oil* ‖ *1 slice fresh ginger root, peeled and finely chopped* ‖ *1 garlic clove, crushed* ‖ *1 teaspoon mixed pepper flakes* ‖ *3 ounces shiitake mushrooms, halved* ‖ *1 red bell pepper, cored, deseeded, and cut into strips* ‖ *1 pound bok choy, halved lengthwise* ‖ *7 ounces fresh baby corn* ‖ *2 tablespoons shoyu or tamari sauce* ‖ *2 teaspoons hot pepper sauce* ‖ *a few drops of sesame oil* ‖ *1 x 14-ounce package firm tofu, cut into ½-inch cubes*

ONE Heat a nonstick sauté pan over a high heat. Add the oil and swirl it around to coat the pan. **TWO** Add the ginger, garlic, and mixed pepper flakes, and stir-fry for a few seconds. **THREE** Toss in the mushrooms and red bell pepper, and stir-fry for a couple of minutes; then add the bok choy and corn and cook for about another 2–3 minutes. Season with the shoyu sauce, pepper sauce, and sesame oil. **FOUR** Add the tofu and mix gently until heated through.

Serves 4 with 2 other main dishes

NUTRIENT ANALYSIS PER SERVING 1059 kJ – 255 cal – 24.9 g protein – 8.3 g carbohydrate – 6.0 g sugar – 13.7 g fat – 1.7 g saturated fat – 6.5 g fiber – 673 mg sodium

HEALTHY TIP Tofu is a valuable source of protein and makes a great alternative to meat in many dishes. It is low in saturated fat and contains vitamin E and some iron and phosphorus.

Lentils with lemon grass and lime leaves

Lentil dishes are rare in traditional Chinese main courses; they are usually used as a stuffing ingredient in rice dumplings wrapped in lotus leaves. This creamy lentil dish is best served with Sticky Rice *(see page 141).*

INGREDIENTS *½ tablespoon canola or olive oil* ‖ *½ tablespoon sesame oil* ‖ *4 shallots, finely sliced* ‖ *2 garlic cloves, crushed* ‖ *2 red chilies, sliced* ‖ *2½ cups Puy or dried brown lentils or yellow mung dhal, washed and rinsed* ‖ *3–4¼ cups Vegetable Stock (see page 17)* ‖ *2 dried kaffir lime leaves* ‖ *2 lemon grass stalks, cut into 1-inch pieces and slightly crushed, plus extra to garnish* ‖ *1 teaspoon grated lemon rind* ‖ *2 tablespoons shoyu or tamari sauce* ‖ *large handful of torn Thai basil leaves (optional)*

ONE Heat the canola and sesame oils in a saucepan over a high heat until hot. Add the shallots, garlic, and chilies, and sauté for a couple of minutes. **TWO** Add the lentils and vegetable stock, and bring to a boil. **THREE** Stir in the lime leaves, lemon grass, lemon rind, and shoyu sauce; then reduce the heat and simmer for about 25–30 minutes, stirring occasionally to prevent the lentils from sticking to the bottom of the pan. Depending on which type of lentils you use, you may need to add more stock so that they don't dry up. Stir in the torn basil leaves, if using. Garnish with the extra lemon grass and serve immediately.

Serves 4–6 with 2 other main dishes

NUTRIENT ANALYSIS PER SERVING 1627 kJ – 384 cal – 32.8 g protein – 56.8 g carbohydrate – 2.7 g sugars – 4.4 g fat – 0.8 g saturated fat – 0.5 g fiber – 267 mg sodium

HEALTHY TIP Lentils are low in fat and are a source of protein and fiber. Unlike meat, fish, poultry, and eggs, they don't contain the ideal amounts of essential amino acids needed for growth and development so should be served with other plant or wholegrain foods, such as rice or bread, to make a "complete" protein.

Quails' eggs with tofu in a creamy peanut sauce

Quails' eggs make an interesting addition to this tofu dish. Some people don't eat tofu because they feel it's too bland, but that's not so in this dish where the tofu takes on a spicy flavor from the creamy peanut sauce. This dish goes well with Steamed Buns *(see page 137)* or boiled egg noodles.

INGREDIENTS *¼ pound small button mushrooms* ‖ *¼ pound shiitake mushrooms, halved* ‖ *3½ ounces canned bamboo shoots, drained* ‖ *1 x 14-ounce pack firm tofu, cut into 1-inch cubes* ‖ *8 quails' eggs, hard-cooked and halved* ‖ *1 tablespoon chopped fresh cilantro, to garnish*

CREAMY PEANUT SAUCE *4 tablespoons reduced-fat peanut butter* ‖ *4 tablespoons Vegetable Stock (see page 17)* ‖ *¼ cup plain soy yogurt* ‖ *3 tablespoons rice wine vinegar* ‖ *1 tablespoon shoyu or tamari sauce* ‖ *1 garlic clove, crushed* ‖ *2 slices fresh ginger root, peeled and finely chopped* ‖ *1 red chili, deseeded and thinly sliced* ‖ *2 tablespoons chopped fresh cilantro*

ONE Make the peanut sauce by whizzing all the ingredients in a food processor until smooth. **TWO** Pour the sauce into a saucepan and heat gently until simmering. Add the button and shiitake mushrooms and the bamboo shoots, and cook gently for 2–3 minutes. Add the tofu cubes and stir gently to warm through. **THREE** Transfer the mixture to a large serving bowl. Arrange the halved quails' eggs over the top and sprinkle with the chopped cilantro.

Serves 4 with 2 other main dishes

NUTRIENT ANALYSIS PER SERVING 645 kJ – 154 cal – 12.9 g protein – 7.5 g carbohydrate – 2.6 g sugar – 8.0 g fat – 1.2 g saturated fat – 1.1 g fiber – 235 mg sodium

HEALTHY TIP Eggs are an excellent source of vitamin B12, an important component for healthy nerves. Many people are concerned about their high cholesterol content (cholesterol is found only in the egg yolk) and its effect on blood cholesterol levels and the risk of heart disease. Heart experts recommend eating no more than 2–3 eggs per week.

Fu yung with vegetables

Fu yung means "pretty face" in Chinese; it is a sort of shirred egg omelet. You can also add cooked meats or shrimp or toasted nuts to the dish, but don't be greedy and add too much or there won't be enough egg to bind the other ingredients. This dish goes well with Sweet and Sour Pork *(see page 53)* and Vegetarian Fried Rice *(see page 138)*.

INGREDIENTS *2 teaspoons canola or olive oil* ‖ *1 scallion, finely sliced* ‖ *2 ounces carrots, cut into 1-inch lengths* ‖ *¼ pound fresh bean sprouts* ‖ *1 cup Chinese flowering chives, cut into 1-inch lengths* ‖ *pinch of coarse sea salt* ‖ *½ teaspoon freshly ground black pepper* ‖ *4 eggs, lightly beaten*

ONE Heat the oil in a nonstick sauté pan over a high heat until piping hot, swirling the oil around the pan. **TWO** Add the scallion and carrots, and stir-fry for a few seconds. Toss in the bean sprouts, Chinese chives, salt and pepper, and stir. **THREE** Pour in the eggs and mix them with the vegetables over a medium to high heat. As the eggs start to set, fold the fu yung over in the middle to form a half-moon shape; then move it back to the center of the pan and continue cooking over a medium to high heat for 2 minutes. Toss or turn it over and cook the other side for 2 minutes. **FOUR** Serve immediately.

Serves 4 with 2 other dishes

NUTRIENT ANALYSIS PER SERVING 487 kJ – 117 cal – 8.5 g protein – 2.5 g carbohydrate – 1.9 g sugars – 8.2 g fat – 2.1 g saturated fat – 1.0 g fiber – 85 mg sodium

HEALTHY TIP In the UK, some eggs are fortified with omega-3 fats, which are usually found only in oily fish. Eating these eggs can be helpful, particularly for people who don't like the taste of oily fish and so miss out on this source of these essential fatty acids.

Apple and fennel salad with tofu and chive dressing

It is rare to find salads on the menus of Chinese restaurants and takeouts. This recipe sets things right by combining the sweetness from the apples with the aniseed flavor of the fennel and rounding it off with a smooth tofu dressing. This salad goes well with Butternut Squash and Tofu Soup *(see page 38)*.

INGREDIENTS *2 sweet red apples, cored and sliced* ‖ *2 Chinese nashi pears, cored and sliced* ‖ *1 large fennel bulb, thinly sliced* ‖ *2 tablespoons toasted walnuts*

TOFU AND CHIVE DRESSING *⅓ cup silken tofu* ‖ *1 tablespoon rice vinegar* ‖ *1 tablespoon apple juice* ‖ *½ garlic clove, crushed* ‖ *2 tablespoons chopped fresh chives*

ONE Blend all the ingredients for the dressing in a food processor. Pour into a screw-top jar and chill until ready to use (it will keep for about a week in the refrigerator). **TWO** Put the apples, pears, and fennel in a salad bowl. Add the dressing and toss until mixed. Sprinkle with the walnuts just before serving.

Serves 4 as a light meal

NUTRIENT ANALYSIS PER SERVING 1492 kJ – 359 cal – 9.8 g protein – 30.1 g carbohydrate – 28.2 g sugar – 22.7 g fat – 1.9 g saturated fat – 7.3 g fiber – 24 mg sodium

HEALTHY TIP Sweet red apples are a good source of vitamin C, which helps to maintain a healthy immune system. In traditional Chinese medicine, apples are used to treat constipation.

Vegetable chop suey

Fresh bean sprouts are the main ingredient in a chop suey dish. You can add whatever other combination of vegetables you like, as long as you don't overcook them. A little of whatever you fancy works brilliantly when making chop suey. The crunchy texture of the different vegetables goes really well with Spareribs *(see page 54)*.

INGREDIENTS *½ tablespoon canola or olive oil* ‖ *1 teaspoon sesame oil* ‖ *1 large shallot, finely sliced* ‖ *1 garlic clove, chopped* ‖ *¼ pound fresh shiitake mushrooms, halved* ‖ *2 ounces canned water chestnuts, drained* ‖ *2 ounces canned bamboo shoots, drained* ‖ *¾ pound fresh bean sprouts* ‖ *2 scallions, cut into ¾-inch lengths* ‖ *2 teaspoons shoyu or tamari sauce* ‖ *½ teaspoon freshly ground black pepper*

ONE Heat the canola and sesame oils in a nonstick sauté pan over a high heat until hot. Add the shallot and garlic, and sauté over a medium heat for 1 minute until fragrant. **TWO** Turn up the heat to high. Add the mushrooms, water chestnuts, and bamboo shoots, and stir-fry for 1 minute. **THREE** Quickly add the bean sprouts, scallions, shoyu sauce, and pepper, and stir-fry for about 30 seconds. Serve immediately.

Serves 4 with 2 other main dishes

NUTRIENT ANALYSIS PER SERVING 242 kJ – 58 cal – 3.6 g protein – 4.9 g carbohydrate – 2.6 g sugar – 2.8 g fat – 0.4 g saturated fat – 1.6 g fiber – 114 mg sodium

HEALTHY TIP Shallots belong to the same family as garlic. In scientific studies, plants from the allium family have been shown to increase the levels of good cholesterol in the body. This good cholesterol helps to carry the bad cholesterol away from the arteries in our bodies and so may help reduce the risk of heart disease.

Bamboo shoots and straw mushrooms with broccoli

Fresh bamboo shoots are often very hard to find outside China, so this recipe makes use of the canned variety. Use bamboo shoot chunks if you can, as they are much crunchier and have a better flavor than the sliced versions. To make a complete vegetarian meal, serve this dish with Quails' Eggs with Tofu in a Creamy Peanut Sauce *(see page 118)*.

INGREDIENTS *1 tablespoon canola or olive oil* ‖ *2 slices fresh ginger root* ‖ *1 garlic clove, crushed* ‖ *1 tablespoon yellow bean sauce* ‖ *1 pound canned bamboo shoot chunks, drained* ‖ *¼ pound canned straw mushrooms* ‖ *6½ tablespoons Vegetable Stock (see page 17)* ‖ *2 tablespoons Chinese rice wine or dry sherry* ‖ *½ pound broccoli florets*

ONE Heat the oil in a nonstick sauté pan or wok over a high heat until piping hot. Add the ginger and garlic, and stir-fry for a few seconds. **TWO** Add the yellow bean sauce and stir-fry for 1 more minute. **THREE** Toss in the bamboo shoots and straw mushrooms, stir and add the stock and rice wine. Braise for about 5 minutes over a medium heat. **FOUR** Turn up the heat. Add the broccoli and stir-fry for about 3–4 minutes, or until most of the stock has evaporated. Serve immediately.

Serves 4 with 2 other main dishes

NUTRIENT ANALYSIS PER SERVING 315 kJ – 76 cal – 5.4 g protein – 3.2 g carbohydrate – 2.5 g sugar – 3.7 g fat – 0.7 g saturated fat – 3.9 g fiber – 170 mg sodium

HEALTHY TIP If you eat this as one of your main dishes, you can notch up two servings of vegetables in one sitting. You will also benefit from an increased intake of fiber, which helps maintain a healthy gut, and enjoy a delicious meal at the same time.

Sea-spiced eggplants

This dish comes from Szechwan and is sometimes referred to as fish-fragrant eggplant because the combination of spices is usually used to cook fish dishes. This version is less spicy than the traditional recipe but equally delicious. Discard the chili seeds if you prefer a mildly flavored dish. It should be served with an equally hearty dish such as Spicy Fish Balls with Sweet and Sour Sauce *(see page 80)*.

INGREDIENTS *1½ pounds eggplants* ‖ *½ tablespoon olive oil* ‖ *4–5 garlic cloves, finely chopped* ‖ *2 slices fresh ginger root, peeled and finely chopped* ‖ *1 red chili, sliced* ‖ *3½ tablespoons Vegetable Stock (see page 17)* ‖ *¾ tablespoon yellow bean sauce* ‖ *1 tablespoon Chinese rice wine or dry sherry* ‖ *1 teaspoon shoyu or tamari sauce* ‖ *2 scallions, chopped, to serve*

CORNSTARCH PASTE *1 teaspoon cornstarch mixed with 1 tablespoon water*

ONE Put the whole eggplants in a foil-lined roasting pan and bake in the center of a preheated oven, 400°F, for 30–35 minutes until they are soft and wrinkly. Remove and set aside to cool; then cut them into 1-inch cubes. **TWO** Heat the oil in a nonstick sauté pan over a high heat until hot. Add the garlic, ginger, and chili, and stir-fry for a few seconds until fragrant. Stir in the stock, yellow bean sauce, rice wine, and shoyu sauce, and bring to a boil. **THREE** Add the eggplant cubes to the sauce and simmer for about 5 minutes. **FOUR** Slowly stir in the cornstarch paste and cook until the sauce has thickened and turned transparent. **FIVE** Sprinkle with the scallions and serve immediately.

Serves 4 with 2 other main dishes

NUTRIENT ANALYSIS PER SERVING 275 kJ – 65 cal – 2.5 g protein – 8.1 g carbohydrate – 4.7 g sugar – 2.4 g fat – 0.4 g saturated fat – 4.2 g fiber – 124 mg sodium

HEALTHY TIP Eggplants can absorb large amounts of oil during cooking. If a recipe calls for eggplant slices, soaking them beforehand in salted water draws out the bitter juices and makes the flesh more dense and less likely to absorb large quantities of fat.

Dry-fried green beans

The Szechwan version of this dish is usually cooked with chili, preserved vegetables, and dried shrimp. This simple recipe dispenses with all these additional ingredients and uses only garlic and rice wine to enhance the natural sweetness of the green beans. Serve with some dim sum dishes, such as Steamed Cashew Nut and Vegetable Dumplings *(see page 36)* and Wonton Soup *(see page 39)* or Rice Congee *(see page 145)* for an unusual Sunday brunch.

INGREDIENTS *½ tablespoon canola or olive oil ‖ 4 garlic cloves, finely chopped ‖ 1 red chili, deseeded and sliced ‖ 1 pound fine green beans, topped and tailed ‖ 1 teaspoon shoyu or tamari sauce ‖ 1 tablespoon Chinese rice wine or dry sherry ‖ 3½ tablespoons Vegetable Stock (see page 17)*

ONE Heat the oil in a nonstick sauté pan over a high heat until hot. Add the garlic and chili, and stir-fry for a few seconds. **TWO** Toss in the green beans and stir-fry for 1 minute; then add the shoyu sauce, rice wine, and vegetable stock. Cover and cook for about 2 minutes. **THREE** Remove the lid and stir-fry the beans for another 1–2 minutes until the stock has evaporated.

Serves 4 with 2 other main dishes

NUTRIENT ANALYSIS PER SERVING 260 kJ – 63 cal – 2.7 g protein – 4.7 g carbohydrate – 3.0 g sugar – 3.4 g fat – 0.5 g saturated fat – 2.9 g fiber – 42 mg sodium

HEALTHY TIP Green beans are a good source of the B group vitamins B1, B2, niacin, and folate, all of which are needed for the release of energy from foods and for the proper functioning of the immune system.

Rice, lentils, and Chinese mushrooms

This mixture of ingredients is often used with fatty pork for the banana leaf dumplings, which are served during the Dragon Boat Festival on the fifth day of the fifth month in the Chinese lunar calendar. This recipe omits the fatty pork and is cooked in a saucepan so it is less laborious and time-consuming but equally delicious.

INGREDIENTS *4–5 dried Chinese mushrooms* ‖ *⅓ cup mung dhal* ‖ *½ pound Thai jasmine rice* ‖ *1 tablespoon canola or olive oil* ‖ *2 shallots, chopped* ‖ *1⅓ cups Vegetable or Chicken Stock (see page 17)* ‖ *5–6 fresh or frozen chestnuts, peeled* ‖ *1 tablespoon chopped fresh cilantro, to garnish (optional)*

ONE Put the dried mushrooms in a heatproof bowl. Cover with boiling water and put a plate on top to keep the steam in. Set aside for 20–30 minutes. Drain the mushrooms and remove the stalks; then squeeze the water out of the caps and cut them in half. **TWO** Wash the mung dhal in several changes of water; then soak for about 10 minutes to soften. Strain and set aside. **THREE** Rinse the rice thoroughly in a sieve and leave to drain. **FOUR** Heat the oil in a saucepan over a medium heat until hot. Add the shallots, cover and sweat for 3–4 minutes over a low heat. **FIVE** Pour in the mung dhal and stir-fry with the shallots for a couple of minutes over a low heat. **SIX** Add the rice and stir to mix. Turn up the heat and pour in the stock. Bring the mixture to a boil; then reduce the heat to its lowest setting. Put the mushrooms and chestnuts on the top of the mixture. Cover and simmer for 15 minutes. **SEVEN** Turn off the heat but leave the rice mixture on the stove top for at least 20 minutes. Serve sprinkled with cilantro leaves, if you like.

Serves 4 as a light meal

NUTRIENT ANALYSIS PER SERVING 1383 kJ – 326 cal – 8.6 g protein – 4.5 g carbohydrate – 1.5 g sugar – 5.6 g fat – 1.1 g saturated fat – 1.1 fiber – 7 mg sodium

HEALTHY TIP Unlike other nuts, chestnuts are high in starchy carbohydrates and fiber but low in fat. They are a good source of vitamin B6, which is needed for the proper functioning of the nervous and immune systems.

Rice and noodles

Stir-fried noodles with peanuts and corn

This recipe takes its inspiration from Southeast Asia, where rice noodles are often eaten as snacks or light lunches rather than as part of a main meal.

INGREDIENTS *¼ pound dried thin rice noodles* ‖ *2 tablespoons canola or olive oil* ‖ *2 garlic cloves, crushed* ‖ *2 slices fresh ginger root, peeled and chopped* ‖ *1 heaped tablespoon medium curry paste* ‖ *½ pound baby corn* ‖ *½ pound conical cabbage, finely sliced* ‖ *1 small red bell pepper, cored, deseeded, and finely sliced* ‖ *½ tablespoon Thai fish sauce* ‖ *2 teaspoons shoyu or tamari sauce* ‖ *4 tablespoons light coconut milk* ‖ *1 cup roughly chopped roasted, unsalted peanuts* ‖ *2 tablespoons chopped fresh cilantro* ‖ *4 scallions, finely sliced* ‖ *2 tablespoons lime juice* ‖ *cilantro sprigs, to garnish*

ONE Put the rice noodles into a bowl of boiling water, cover and leave to stand for 5 minutes for them to soften. Drain and set aside. **TWO** Heat the oil in a large nonstick sauté pan over a high heat until piping hot. Add the garlic, ginger, and curry paste, and stir-fry for 2–3 minutes until the spices become fragrant. **THREE** Add the corn, cabbage, and red bell pepper, and stir-fry for about 5 minutes, or until the cabbage has started to soften and wilt. **FOUR** Add the fish sauce, shoyu sauce, and coconut milk. Stir to mix, then toss in the rice noodles and stir-fry until the noodles have warmed through. Turn off the heat and gently stir in the peanuts, cilantro leaves, scallions, and lime juice. Garnish with cilantro sprigs.

Serves 4

NUTRIENT ANALYSIS PER SERVING 2272 kJ – 557 cal – 18.7 g protein – 72.0 g carbohydrate – 10.7 g sugars – 22.8 g fat – 4.5 g saturated fat – 7.0 g fiber – 464 mg sodium

HEALTHY TIP Corn contains two important plant chemicals, zeaxanthin and lutein. Scientific studies have shown that both act as antioxidants, which fight against damaging free radicals, particularly in the eyes.

Chicken chow mein

Chow mein literally means fried noodles. In this dish the crispy, browned noodles soak up the sauce from the chicken and bean sprout topping. If you like, you can spice it up with chili sauce.

INGREDIENTS *7 ounces chicken breast, cut into thin strips* ‖ *7½ ounces whole-wheat or egg noodles* ‖ *1 tablespoon canola or olive oil* ‖ *2 garlic cloves, sliced* ‖ *2 teaspoons shoyu or tamari sauce* ‖ *1¼ cups hot Chicken Stock (see page 17)* ‖ *½ pound fresh bean sprouts* ‖ *2 scallions, sliced*

MARINADE *½ teaspoon cornstarch* ‖ *½ teaspoon sesame oil* ‖ *freshly ground white pepper*

CORNSTARCH PASTE *2 teaspoons cornstarch mixed with 2 tablespoons water*

ONE Mix together the marinade ingredients and rub the mixture into the chicken strips. Set aside. **TWO** Put the noodles into a large bowl of boiling water. Cover and leave to stand for 5–8 minutes, or until they are soft. Drain and set aside. **THREE** Heat ½ tablespoon of the oil in a nonstick sauté pan over a high heat. Add the garlic and stir-fry for a few seconds until slightly browned. **FOUR** Add the noodles with 1 teaspoon of the shoyu sauce and fry until crispy. Transfer to a serving plate. **FIVE** Heat the remaining oil in the same pan. Add the chicken strips and stir-fry until they are almost cooked; then add the hot stock and the remaining shoyu sauce and cook for 1 minute. **SIX** Toss in the bean sprouts and scallions and stir-fry for 1 more minute. **SEVEN** Slowly add the cornstarch paste and stir to thicken the sauce. Cook until the sauce has turned transparent, then pour it over the crispy noodles.

Serves 4 as a light snack

NUTRIENT ANALYSIS PER SERVING 1445 kJ – 342 cal – 21.0 g protein – 45.7 g carbohydrate – 2.6 g sugar – 9.7 g fat – 2.1 g saturated fat – 2.7 g fiber – 220 mg sodium

HEALTHY TIP Garlic is used a lot in oriental cuisine. Its health benefits have been touted for hundreds of years, yet it's only recently that some of these benefits have undergone scientific scrutiny. For example, research has shown that garlic has a beneficial effect on the way our blood clots, which has important implications for maintaining heart health.

Herby rice noodle soup with cashew nuts

Flat rice noodles (ho fun) are made from rice flour, wheat starch, and water. It's often difficult to find fresh ho fun outside an oriental supermarket, so this recipe uses dried rice noodles instead. They taste just as good, but can easily be overcooked and become soft and mushy.

INGREDIENTS *7½ ounces dried medium rice noodles (ho fun)* ‖ *3¾ pints Vegetable Stock (see page 17)* ‖ *1 tablespoon shoyu or tamari sauce* ‖ *2 scallions, sliced diagonally* ‖ *2 tablespoons chopped fresh cilantro* ‖ *2 tablespoons chopped fresh mint* ‖ *¼ pound fresh bean sprouts* ‖ *⅓ cup roasted, unsalted cashew nuts* ‖ *½ teaspoon sesame oil* ‖ *1 lime, cut into wedges*

ONE Bring a large saucepan of water to a boil. Add the rice noodles, turn off the heat, and cover the pan. Leave to steam for about 3–4 minutes; then drain. **TWO** Meanwhile, bring the vegetable stock to a boil. Add the shoyu sauce, reduce the heat, and leave to simmer until ready to use. **THREE** Divide the rice noodles among 4 large bowls and top with the scallions, cilantro, mint, bean sprouts, and cashew nuts. **FOUR** Divide the hot stock among the 4 bowls and serve immediately with the lime wedges.

Serves 4 as a light snack

NUTRIENT ANALYSIS PER SERVING 1255 kJ – 301 cal – 6.2 g protein – 54.7 g carbohydrate – 1.4 g sugar – 5.5 g fat – 1.0 g saturated fat – 0.9 g fiber – 137 mg sodium

HEALTHY TIP Like all citrus fruit, limes are an excellent source of vitamin C. Lime juice makes a good alternative to salt, which is useful if you're trying to cut down on the amount of salt in your diet.

Rice noodles with aromatic shrimp

Rice noodles are very versatile and can be fried, served in soup, or used to soak up the flavors from aromatic spices and shrimp, as in this dish. They make a good alternative to boiled rice with a main meal.

INGREDIENTS *¾ pound raw shrimp, patted dry with kitchen paper towel* ‖ *2 tablespoons olive oil* ‖ *¾ pound dried thin rice noodles* ‖ *4 garlic cloves, chopped* ‖ *3 red chilies, deseeded and chopped* ‖ *2 lemon grass stalks, finely chopped* ‖ *2 onions, shredded lengthwise* ‖ *6 celery stalks, shredded lengthwise* ‖ *4 teaspoons shoyu or tamari sauce* ‖ *3 scallions, shredded lengthwise* ‖ *3 tablespoons Lemon and Fish Sauce (see page 19)* ‖ *freshly ground black pepper* ‖ *4 tablespoons crushed roasted unsalted peanuts, to serve* ‖ *2 red chilies, split lengthwise to garnish*

ONE Mix the shrimp with 1 tablespoon of the olive oil a small bowl and set aside. **TWO** Soak the rice noodles in hot water to cover. Leave for about 5–10 minutes until soft. Drain well, transfer to a serving plate, and keep warm. **THREE** Heat a nonstick pan until very hot. Add the shrimp and sear on each side for about 30 seconds until golden brown. Remove from the pan and set aside. **FOUR** Heat the remaining oil, swirling it around to coat the pan. Add the garlic, chilies, and lemon grass, and stir-fry for about 30 seconds until the garlic is lightly browned. Toss in the onions and celery, and stir-fry for a couple of minutes, until they have softened a little. **FIVE** Return the shrimp to the pan. Add the shoyu sauce and scallions, and season with pepper. Arrange on top of the noodles and drizzle with the Lemon and Fish Sauce. **SIX** To serve, sprinkle with the crushed peanuts and garnish with the red chilies. Serve the remaining sauce in a pitcher.

Serves 4 as a light main meal

NUTRIENT ANALYSIS PER SERVING 2599 kJ – 622 cal – 28.4 g protein – 93.1 g carbohydrate – 7.3 g sugar – 14.0 g fat – 2.2 g saturated fat – 2.8 g fiber – 793 mg sodium

HEALTHY TIP Celery contains a plant chemical called apigenin, which has anti-inflammatory properties, so it may help to alleviate the painful symptoms of gout. It is also a good source of soluble fiber, which may help to lower blood cholesterol.

Buckwheat noodles with cashew nuts and cilantro

This recipe is a simplified version of laksa, a spicy Malaysian noodle soup, but it is made with buckwheat noodles, which are denser than the traditional rice noodles.

INGREDIENTS ¾ pound buckwheat or soba noodles ‖ ½ tablespoon canola or olive oil ‖ ½ teaspoon sesame oil ‖ 1 large onion, thinly sliced ‖ 4 garlic cloves, crushed ‖ 1 large carrot, thinly sliced ‖ 1 slice fresh ginger root, peeled and finely chopped ‖ 1 red chili, deseeded and sliced ‖ 4½ pints Vegetable Stock (see page 17) ‖ 4 tablespoons tamarind paste ‖ 3 tablespoons shoyu or tamari sauce

TO SERVE 1¼ cups unsalted, roasted cashew nuts ‖ handful of chopped fresh cilantro

ONE Put the buckwheat noodles in a large pan of boiling water. Cover the pan, turn off the heat, and leave the noodles to steam for 5–7 minutes until slightly softened. Drain in a colander and set aside. **TWO** Meanwhile, heat the two canola and sesame oils in a large saucepan over a medium to high heat. Add the onion, garlic, carrot, ginger, and chili, and cook for 2–3 minutes, stirring occasionally. **THREE** Add the stock and tamarind paste, and bring to a boil. Reduce the heat and simmer for about 10 minutes, then add the shoyu sauce. **FOUR** Divide the buckwheat noodles among 4–6 bowls and spoon the broth over the top. **FIVE** To serve, sprinkle with the cashew nuts and chopped cilantro.

Serves 4–6 as a main meal

NUTRIENT ANALYSIS PER SERVING 2533 kJ – 607 cal – 20.8 g protein – 90.4 g carbohydrate – 19.9 g sugar – 20.8 g fat – 4.0 g saturated fat – 2.4 g fiber – 1068 mg sodium

HEALTHY TIP Soba or buckwheat noodles are Japanese and contain more fiber than rice noodles. Look out for ones made with green tea (cha soba). Tea contains a plant nutrient called quercetin, which acts as a strong antioxidant. Research among the Japanese has shown a lower incidence of cancer among tea drinkers, particularly those who drink green tea.

Steamed buns

The northern Chinese eat buns and dumplings as their main source of carbohydrate. In Szechwan, steamed buns are traditionally made with lard, but in this recipe olive oil is used instead. These buns can be served as an accompaniment to a main meal or as a snack.

INGREDIENTS *½ teaspoon dried yeast* ‖ *1 teaspoon sugar* ‖ *¾ cup warm water* ‖ *2¼ cups all-purpose flour* ‖ *1 tablespoon olive oil* ‖ *20 small squares of wax paper*

ONE Put the dried yeast and sugar in a bowl. Add the warm water, stir and leave in a warm place until the yeast becomes frothy. **TWO** Sift the flour into a large mixing bowl. Add the yeast mixture and the oil, and stir to mix. **THREE** Using your hands, work the mixture into a dough; you may need to add extra flour if the dough is too sticky to work with. Transfer it to a lightly floured surface and knead for about 5 minutes until the dough is smooth. **FOUR** Return the dough to the bowl. Cover with a damp dish towel and leave to rise in a warm place for about 1½ hours, or until the dough has doubled in size. **FIVE** Lightly punch the dough down for a few seconds, then divide it into 20 pieces. Roll them into whatever shape you fancy—balls, knots, crescents, for example—and put each one on a square of wax paper to prevent them from sticking. Leave for 15 minutes to rise again. **SIX** Meanwhile, fill a wok two-thirds full of water, set a wok rack in the middle, and bring the water to a boil. Steam the buns in a large bamboo steamer, on high heat for about 10–12 minutes. Remove from the heat and serve immediately.

Makes 20 buns

NUTRIENT ANALYSIS PER BUN 226 kJ – 53 cal – 1.4 g protein – 11.0 g carbohydrate – 0.5 g sugar – 0.7 g fat – 0.1 g saturated fat – 0.4 g fiber – trace sodium

HEALTHY TIP By replacing a quarter of the amount of all-purpose flour with wholemeal flour, you can double the fiber content of these buns. The plain buns can be frozen; to reheat, steam them for 10 minutes over a high heat.

Vegetarian fried rice

This is a colorful and flavorsome way of using up leftover boiled rice. Special fried rice, which contains meat and shrimp that increase the protein content, is often found on takeout menus. This lighter version relies on crunchy vegetables. This dish goes well with Roast Pork *(see page 56)*.

INGREDIENTS *1 tablespoon olive oil* ‖ *1¼ cups diced carrots* ‖ *1 beaten egg* ‖ *1 pound hot boiled white rice cooked in Vegetable Stock (see page 140)* ‖ *¾ cup defrosted frozen peas* ‖ *½ cup canned corn kernels, drained* ‖ *3½ ounces canned pineapple chunks, drained* ‖ *1 tablepoon shoyu or tamari sauce* ‖ *½ teaspoon white pepper* ‖ *2 tablespoons chopped scallions, to serve*

ONE Heat the oil in a nonstick wok or sauté pan and stir-fry the carrots for 1 minute; then add the beaten egg. **TWO** Add the cooked rice, peas, corn, and pineapple, and stir-fry for about 5 minutes. Season with shoyu sauce and white pepper. **THREE** To serve, mix in the chopped scallions.

Serves 4 as an accompaniment to a main meal

NUTRIENT ANALYSIS PER SERVING 1572 kJ – 371 cal – 9.4 g protein – 71.1 g carbohydrate – 9.0 g sugars – 7.5 g fat – 1.6 g saturated fat – 2.8 g fiber – 226 mg sodium

HEALTHY TIP Pineapple contains a good supply of vitamin C, fiber, and potassium.

Boiled rice

Rice is the staple food in southern China. Many people think that boiled rice is bland, but that is not so in this recipe, where stock is used instead of water to enhance the taste. Remember that rice should not be cooked like pasta. Under no circumstances should it be rinsed under cold water after cooking to separate the grains of rice.

INGREDIENTS *¾ pound Thai jasmine or long-grain rice* ‖ *1¼ cups Vegetable or Chicken Stock (see page 17)*

ONE Put the rice in a sieve and wash it under running warm water, rubbing the grains together between your hands. This gets rid of any excess starch. **TWO** Put the rice into a saucepan and add the stock. Place the pan on the smallest ring on the stove top and bring it to a boil. Give it a quick stir, then reduce the heat to a simmer. Cover with a lid and leave to cook for 15 minutes. Turn off the heat and let the rice steam with the lid on for another 20 minutes. Don't be tempted to lift the lid to check what's going on. **THREE** To serve, fluff up the grains of rice with a spoon or fork.

Serves 4 as an accompaniment to a main meal

NUTRIENT ANALYSIS PER SERVING 1314 kJ – 314 cal – 6.5 g protein – 70.0 g carbohydrate – 0 g sugar – 0.4 g fat – 0 g saturated fat – 0 g fiber – 0 mg sodium

HEALTHY TIP Rice has been used traditionally in Chinese medicine to treat a range of intestinal problems, from indigestion to stomach ulcers. To increase the fiber content of this dish, replace a quarter of the white rice with brown rice. This gives it an extra crunchy, nutty flavor.

Sticky rice

You can buy sticky or glutinous rice from oriental supermarkets. The grains are white and short, and when they are cooked, they turn transparent and glutinous. If you're really stuck, Japanese sushi rice make a reasonable alternative.

INGREDIENTS *1½ cups glutinous rice* ‖ *1½ pints water*

ONE Wash the rice in several changes of water and drain. Put it in a large mixing bowl. Cover with plenty of cold water and leave to soak for about 5–6 hours, or overnight. **TWO** Drain the rice and wash it again; then drain thoroughly. **THREE** Heat some water in the bottom of a double boiler. Place the rice in the top pan and pour in enough water to reach about ½ inch above the rice. Cover and steam on a low heat for about 20–30 minutes. Remember to check the level of water in the bottom of the double boiler to prevent burning. If you don't have a double boiler, you can improvise by putting the soaked glutinous rice in a metal vegetable steamer and placing this over a saucepan of boiling water. Cover and steam for about 1 hour. You will need to check the water levels periodically to check that the saucepan hasn't boiled dry.

Serves 4 as an accompaniment to a main meal

NUTRIENT ANALYSIS PER SERVING 1127 kJ – 269 cal – 6.3 g protein – 56.2 g carbohydrate – 0 g sugar – 1.2 g fat – 0 g saturated fat – 0 g fiber – 2 mg sodium

HEALTHY TIP Sticky rice makes a good alternative to regular boiled rice to serve with a meal. You can add corn, carrots, peas, and cooked meats to make this dish into a nutritious snack or light lunch.

Shrimp fried rice

This colorful fried rice recipe is my version of a very popular dish found on the menus of all Chinese restaurants and takeouts—special fried rice. This recipe doesn't include eggs or pork; instead it contains shrimp and an assortment of vegetables.

INGREDIENTS *1 tablespoon canola or olive oil* ‖ *1 pound fresh shrimp, peeled and deveined* ‖ *2 ounces shiitake or button mushrooms, halved* ‖ *1 zucchini, thinly sliced* ‖ *1 small carrot, thinly sliced* ‖ *2 ounces green beans, cut into 1-inch pieces* ‖ *1 pound hot Boiled Rice (see page 140)* ‖ *2 teaspoons shoyu or tamari sauce* ‖ *1 teaspoon freshly ground black pepper* ‖ *1 scallion, thinly sliced, to serve*

ONE Heat the oil in a nonstick sauté pan until piping hot and stir-fry the shrimp for 1 minute over a high heat. Remove the shrimp and set aside. **TWO** Add the mushrooms, zucchini, carrot, and green beans, and stir-fry for a couple of minutes over a high heat. **THREE** Stir in the hot rice and shoyu sauce. Season with pepper and mix thoroughly. **FOUR** Return the shrimp to the pan and stir-fry the rice mixture for 2 minutes. **FIVE** To serve, sprinkle with the scallion.

Serves 2 as a main meal or 4 with 2 other dishes

NUTRIENT ANALYSIS PER SERVING 2690 kJ – 636 cal – 49.3 g protein – 90.5 g carbohydrate – 4.6 g sugar – 11.1 g fat – 2.0 g saturated fat – 2.6 g fiber – 609 mg sodium

HEALTHY TIP Shiitake mushrooms contain a special type of carbohydrate called lentinan. Trials have shown that extracts of lentinan can boost the immune system and thus increase our resistance to infections.

Chinese pancakes

These are sometimes called Mandarin pancakes and are used to accompany Crispy Aromatic Duck *(see page 24).* Chinese pancakes can be bought ready-made in most supermarkets, but this recipe is very simple, and the pancakes can be made ahead and stored in the refrigerator or frozen until required.

INGREDIENTS *2 cups all-purpose flour* ‖ *¾ cup boiling water* ‖ *1 tablespoon sesame oil*

ONE Sift the flour into a large mixing bowl. Slowly add a boiling water, beating it in with a fork or a pair of chopsticks. Add more water if necessary. **TWO** Remove the dough from the bowl and knead until it is smooth and elastic. Return the dough to the mixing bowl. Cover with a damp dish towel and leave to rest for about 30 minutes. **THREE** Knead the dough for 2–3 minutes, then form it into a long roll about 2 inches in diameter. Divide it into 16 pieces. Roll each piece into a thin pancake about 6 inches in diameter. **FOUR** Brush the top of 2 pancakes with some sesame oil and sandwich them together with the oiled surfaces facing inward. Repeat until all the pancakes have been sandwiched together. You should now have 8 pairs of pancakes. **FIVE** Heat a nonstick sauté pan over a low heat until hot. Add a double pancake and cook for 2–3 minutes on one side (brown spots should appear on the bottom as the pancake is cooked); then turn it over and cook the other side for 2 minutes. Remove and cool slightly. **SIX** Pull the two pancakes apart and fold each one in half and half again. Stack them on a heatproof dish and keep them warm while you are cooking the remaining pancakes. These pancakes will keep in the refrigerator for 2–3 days. To reheat them, steam for about 5 minutes over a high heat.

Makes 16 pancakes

NUTRIENT ANALYSIS PER PANCAKE 232 kJ – 55 cal – 1.3 g protein – 10.9 g carbohydrate – 0.2 g sugar – 0.9 g fat – 0.1 g saturated fat – 0.4 g fiber – trace sodium

HEALTHY TIP These pancakes can be stuffed with a range of ingredients, from raw vegetables to boiled eggs and lettuce. Include them in your child's lunchbox as an alternative to a regular sandwich. If you replace a quarter of the white flour with wholemeal, you can discreetly increase the fiber content without a noticeable difference in taste.

Rice congee

Rice congee or porridge is easy to make. It is often thought of as comfort food and has a huge fan base, ranging from young children to convalescents. This recipe uses leftover cooked rice. You can add whatever ingredients you fancy—some people like it with cooked chicken and scallions or preserved duck eggs, while others prefer it plain and treat it more like a soothing soup to accompany a plate of noodles or dim sum.

INGREDIENTS *1¾ pints Vegetable or Chicken Stock (see page 17)* ‖ *7½ ounces cooked rice*

ONE Bring the stock to a boil in a large heavy saucepan on the smallest ring on the stove top. **TWO** Add the cooked rice, stir and partially cover the pan with the lid. Simmer for 30–45 minutes over the lowest heat, stirring occasionally to prevent the rice from sticking to the bottom of the pan.

Serves 4 as a light breakfast or snack

NUTRIENT ANALYSIS PER SERVING 294 kJ – 69 cal – 1.2 g protein – 16.7 g carbohydrate – 0 g sugar – 0.2 g fat – 0 g saturated fat – 0.1 g fiber – 1 mg sodium

HEALTHY TIP Rice or faan is the staple food of southern China. It is a good source of carbohydrates and is gluten-free. Because the bran is removed to make white rice, many of the vitamins and minerals are lost during the refining process, but you can now buy vitamin-enriched white rice. The healthiest alternative is, of course, brown or wholegrain rice, but often the Chinese will not treat this as a staple ingredient. If you gradually substitute small quantities of brown rice for white rice, you may come to prefer it.

Desserts

Tapioca pudding with coconut milk

Tapioca is sometimes used in Chinese dessert soups, which many people from the West say are an acquired taste. In this recipe, it is used to make a pudding, providing a background for the more intense flavors of mango and coconut milk.

INGREDIENTS *4½ pints water* ‖ *1 cup pearl tapioca* ‖ *2 tablespoons elderflower cordial* ‖ *¾ cup light coconut milk* ‖ *¾ cup mango juice* ‖ *1 large mango, peeled, pitted, and sliced*

ONE Bring the water to a boil in a saucepan. Add the tapioca and cook for about 20 minutes, or until the tapioca is transparent. **TWO** Strain the cooked tapioca and divide it among ⅔-cup jelly molds. Chill in the refrigerator for about 2 hours until set. **THREE** Mix the elderflower cordial, coconut milk, and mango juice in bowl. **FOUR** Unmold the tapioca puddings into individual bowls. Spoon the coconut mixture over the top and serve the sliced mango on the side.

Serves 4

NUTRIENT ANALYSIS PER SERVING 739 kJ – 215 cal – 0.5 g protein – 46.1 g carbohydrate – 10.1 g sugars – 4.2g fat – 3.7 g saturated fat – 1.1 g fiber – 27 mg sodium

HEALTHY TIP Mango is a rich source of both beta carotene, which can be converted into vitamin A by the body, and vitamin C. Both these vitamins act as antioxidants, which help to protect the body against damage by free radicals, which are believed to cause some cancers and heart disease.

Almond jelly with assorted fruits

Soy milk is used in this Chinese dessert instead of the traditional evaporated milk, which makes it lower in fat and calories. As it is made with agar agar instead of gelatine, it is suitable for vegetarians.

INGREDIENTS *4¼ cups water* ‖ *¼ ounce agar agar, cut up* ‖ *¼ cup superfine sugar* ‖ *¾ cup soy milk* ‖ *2 teaspoons almond extract* ‖ *½ pound assorted fruits (e.g., mango, melon, kiwi fruit, and physalis), chopped*

ONE Bring the water to a boil in a saucepan; then reduce the heat and add the agar agar. Let it dissolve slowly (it will take about 20 minutes), stirring occasionally. **TWO** Add the sugar and stir until dissolved. Remove the pan from the heat. **THREE** Stir in the soy milk; then strain the mixture through a fine sieve into a mixing bowl. **FOUR** Stir in the almond extract. Pour into 6 x ⅔-cup jelly molds and chill for about an hour until set. **FIVE** To serve, unmold the jelly onto a serving dish and arrange the fruit around it.

Serves 6

NUTRIENT ANALYSIS PER SERVING 246 kJ – 58 cal – 1.0 g protein – 13.0 g carbohydrate – 12.4 g sugars – 0.6 g fat – 0.1 g saturated fat – 1.7 g fiber – 15 mg sodium

HEALTHY TIP Serving an assortment of fruits ensures that we top up on a variety of vitamins and minerals. For example, mangos contain beta carotene, which is needed for healthy sight; kiwifruit is an excellent source of vitamin C (a single fruit contains more than the daily adult requirement); and physalis (Chinese lantern) helps maintain a healthy blood pressure.

Coconut pancakes with fruit

These light, fluffy pancakes are made with rice flour instead of wheat flour. The addition of reduced-fat coconut milk make these a firm family favorite, particularly if you enlist the help of kids in the preparation of the batter and let them stuff their own pancakes.

INGREDIENTS *⅔ cup canned reduced-fat coconut milk ‖ ¾ cup rice flour ‖ ⅔ cup mango juice ‖ 2 tablespoons canola or olive oil, for frying ‖ 10 ounces assorted fruits (e.g., papaya, pineapple, and kiwi fruit), chopped ‖ 1 tablespoon toasted pumpkin seeds*

ONE Make the pancake batter. Combine the coconut milk, rice flour, and mango juice in a bowl. Beat well, then leave the batter to stand for about 15 minutes. **TWO** Put ½ teaspoon oil in a small nonstick frying pan, about 6 inches across, and heat over a medium heat until piping hot, swirling the oil around the pan. **THREE** Spoon a thin layer of batter into the frying pan and cook until the top has set. Flip the pancake and cook the other side for about a minute. Remove the pancake and keep warm. Repeat until all the batter has been used, using ½ teaspoon oil for frying each pancake. **FOUR** To serve, put some of the fresh fruit in the middle of each pancake and roll it up. Scatter the pumpkin seeds over the top and serve immediately.

Makes 6 pancakes

NUTRIENT ANALYSIS PER PANCAKE 517 kJ – 147 cal – 2.1 g protein – 21.7 g carbohydrate – 7.7 g sugars – 5.6 g fat – 2.6 g saturated fat – 1.4 g fiber – 17 mg sodium

HEALTHY TIP Pumpkin seeds make a nutritious addition to these pancakes. They are a useful source of iron, which is needed for healthy blood, and of zinc, which is required for growth and the development of a healthy immune system.

Lychee slush

Lychees are Chinese fruit that are in season between November and January. They have a wonderful perfume and are best eaten fresh, but because of their short season this recipe uses canned ones. This recipe was inspired by fruit sorbets, but because lychees are naturally very sweet, there is no added sugar.

INGREDIENTS *1 pound 2 ounce can lychees in natural juice* ‖ *1 teaspoon finely grated fresh ginger root* ‖ *1 teaspoon finely grated lemon grass stalk* ‖ *5 tablespoons water* ‖ *½ cup lemon juice*

ONE Drain the lychees and reserve the liquid. **TWO** Whizz the lychees, ginger, and lemon grass in a food processor until smooth. **THREE** Combine the water, the reserved lychee liquid, and the lemon juice in a saucepan over a medium heat. Add the puréed lychee mixture to the pan. Stir to mix and heat to simmering point; then remove from heat and leave to cool. **FOUR** Pour the mixture into a freezer container, about 8 x 12 inches. Cover and freeze, stirring occasionally, until just firm, which will take about 1 hour.

Serves 4

NUTRIENT ANALYSIS PER SERVING 425 kJ – 599 cal – 0.7 g protein – 25.7g carbohydrate – 25.6 g sugars – trace fat – 0 g saturated fat – 0.7 g fiber – 3 mg sodium

HEALTHY TIP Fresh lychees are an excellent source of vitamin C, which helps to fight infection and boost the immune system. Canned lychees also contain vitamin C, but not as much as the fresh fruit.

Tropical fruit platter

Traditionally, a Chinese meal ends with sliced oranges, which is a good way to include a portion of fruit as a matter of routine rather than effort. This recipe lists some fruit you might like to serve at the end of a meal on a hot summer day. I sometimes serve it with Lychee Slush (see opposite), and sometimes I like to serve these fruits on banana leaves over a bed of ice.

INGREDIENTS *1 pineapple* ‖ *1 papaya* ‖ *2 kiwifruit* ‖ *2 star fruits (carambola)* ‖ *12 kumquats* ‖ *¼ pound strawberries* ‖ *¼ pound blackberries* ‖ *fresh mint leaves, to decorate*

ONE Chill all the fruits until cold. **TWO** When you are ready to serve, peel the pineapple, remove the core, and cut it into large cubes. Peel the papaya, scoop out the seeds, and slice lengthwise. Peel the kiwifruit and cut into slices. Cut the star fruits into ¾-inch slices. **THREE** To serve, arrange the fruit on a large serving platter and scatter with mint leaves.

Serves 6

NUTRIENT ANALYSIS PER SERVING 264 kJ – 62 cal – 1.1 g protein – 14.3 g carbohydrate – 0.4 g fat – trace saturated fat – 3.0 g fiber – 6 mg sodium

HEALTHY TIP Strawberries and blackberries are excellent sources of vitamin C, and blackberries also contain plant chemicals called anthocyanides, which act as antioxidants, helping to mop up damaging free radicals from the body. Papaya also contains vitamin C; half a papaya meets the daily adult vitamin C requirement. Kiwifruit is an excellent source of potassium and vitamin C.

Sesame bananas

Many people like to end their meal in a Chinese restaurant with sesame toffee bananas, which are high in calories. In this low-fat variation, the bananas are baked with apple juice, which provides a natural alternative to the sweetness of caramelized sugar in the traditional version.

INGREDIENTS *1 pint apple juice* ‖ *½ teaspoon ground cinnamon* ‖ *½ teaspoon coconut extract* ‖ *4 bananas, chopped into large chunks* ‖ *½ cup plain soy yogurt* ‖ *1 tablespoon toasted sesame seeds*

ONE Combine the apple juice, cinnamon, and coconut extract in a saucepan. Bring the mixture to a boil; then reduce the heat and simmer for 5 minutes. **TWO** Add the bananas, cover the pan, and simmer for about 10 minutes, or until the bananas are soft. Remove them with a slotted spoon and divide among 4 dessert bowls. **THREE** Stir the yogurt into the apple juice mixture to make a thick sauce. To serve, spoon the sauce over the bananas and sprinkle with sesame seeds.

Serves 4

NUTRIENT ANALYSIS PER SERVING 775 kJ – 182 cal – 2.5 g protein – 39.5 g carbohydrate – 36.9 g sugars – 2.7 g fat – 0.4 g saturated fat – 1.4 g fiber – 11 mg sodium

HEALTHY TIP Bananas are an excellent source of potassium, which is needed for the proper functioning of the nerves and muscles.

Avocado and coconut smoothie

The avocado makes this smoothie creamy and delicious. Its vivid green will entice even the youngest family members to try it.

INGREDIENTS *1 cup calcium-fortified soy milk* ‖ *¾ cup soy yogurt* ‖ *1 large ripe avocado, pitted and diced* ‖ *2 tablespoons canned reduced-fat coconut milk*

ONE Whizz the soy milk, yogurt, and avocado in a blender until smooth. **TWO** Divide the smoothie between 2 tall glasses and top with a tablespoon of coconut milk. Serve immediately.

Serves 2

NUTRIENT ANALYSIS PER SERVING 1201 kJ – 303 cal – 6.9 g protein – 14.7 g carbohydrate – 12.3 g sugars – 24.2 g fat – 5.9 g saturated fat – 3.5 g fiber – 94 mg sodium

HEALTHY TIP Avocados are a good source of vitamin E and potassium, and also contain vitamins B1, B6, and C. Like olive oil, they are rich in monounsaturated fats, which are thought to help lower blood cholesterol levels. Avocados are a good source of fat, but even though they contain good fats, they are high in calories.

Red bean smoothie

Red beans are an unusual ingredient in this smoothie recipe. This drink can be filling, so it makes a great afternoon snack if you're feeling peckish after a light lunch.

INGREDIENTS *4¼ cups water ‖ ¼ pound red aduki beans, soaked in water for 4 hours and drained ‖ 2¼ cups calcium-fortified soy milk ‖ 3 tablespoons canned reduced-fat coconut milk ‖ crushed ice*

ONE Bring the water to a boil in a saucepan. Add the aduki beans and simmer over a low heat for 1–1½ hours until the beans are cooked. Remove from the heat and leave to cool. **TWO** Whizz the aduki beans and soy milk in a blender until smooth. **THREE** Divide the red bean mixture among 2–3 tall glasses and spoon some coconut milk over the top of each one. Add some crushed ice just before serving.

Serves 2–3

NUTRIENT ANALYSIS PER SERVING 601 kJ – 152 cal – 10.3 g protein – 19.2 g carbohydrate – 3.4 g sugars – 4.3 g fat – 1.4 g saturated fat – 3.5 g fiber – 80 mg sodium

HEALTHY TIP Pulses such as aduki beans are low in fat as well as being good sources of protein and fiber. Pulses contain both soluble and insoluble fiber, which means that they can help to maintain a healthy gut as well as having the ability to help lower blood cholesterol levels.

Index

Author acknowledgments

I would like to thank my family and friends who, over the years, have shared recipes, tips and many wonderful meals with me; in particular my father Wai Man Chan, husband Pak Sham and dear friends Dominic Lam and Brian Oliver. Thanks must also go to Brenda Wong and Eddie Chan at the Chinese Healthy Living Centre, Simon Lam and Thomas Chan at the Chinese Takeaway Association, and Sue Burke at William Levene. Finally, I am most grateful to Ken Hom, the author of my first-ever and favourite cookbook, for his encouragement and for writing the foreword.

The author and publisher would like to thank Blue Dragon for providing ingredients for the photography. For further information visit: www.bluedragon.com

EXECUTIVE EDITOR Nicky Hill

PROJECT EDITOR Jessica Cowie

EXECUTIVE ART EDITOR AND DESIGN Geoff Fennell

PHOTOGRAPHY William Reavell / © Octopus Publishing Group Ltd

ASSISTANT PRODUCTION CONTROLLER Aileen O'Reilly

FOOD STYLIST Tonia George